To Brian

We hope this is
really helpful for you
We send it with love

Cathy [illegible]

To Brian –
always know that you are a key
part of the Transformation. The
pure field is love. Peace to you.

John [illegible]

Praise for *Spiritual Prescriptions for Turbulent Times*

"At last … a book that heralds the new era of Energy Psychology with a commonsense prescription for holistic health. Cathy and Leslie have masterfully woven science, spirituality, and life stories together to share powerful healing techniques for body, mind, and spirit. Personal transformation is possible by following the advice shared in this book. A magical prescription for your personal holistic healing is right here for the taking!"—Deb Selway, PhD, author, *Women of Spirit*

"*Spiritual Prescriptions for Turbulent Times* is a wise and practical how-to guide for transforming your energy and raising your personal vibration. It offers an approach to healing yourself that is the basis for healing the world."—Marci Shimoff, #1 *New York Times* bestselling author, *Happy for No Reason, Love for No Reason, Chicken Soup for the Woman's Soul*

"In *Spiritual Prescriptions for Turbulent Times* two experienced psychotherapists courageously venture outside the psychotherapeutic box and invite you to explore and heal your emotional pain through powerful non-traditional methods and holistic tools. *Spiritual Prescriptions* is a perfect guide to use on your own or as an adjunct to psychotherapy. Beautifully written, practical and timely!"—Gloria Hemsher, co-author, *Psychic Psychology: Energy Skills for Life and Relationships* and *Basic Psychic Development: A User's Guide to Auras, Chakras and Clairvoyance*

"I have seen these methods lead to significant breakthroughs for patients who had been unable to move forward in their therapy. These authors have gathered the best healing tools available and offer them as a gift to those who wish to grow emotionally and spiritually, either on your own or in psychotherapy."—Tammy Wilkins, MD, adult psychiatrist

"*Spiritual Prescriptions for Turbulent Times* reminds us all that we are here for a reason and we all play a part in transforming our world from chaos to peace."—Janet Bray Attwood, co-author, *New York Times* bestseller *The Passion Test: The Effortless Path to Discovering Your Life Purpose*

Spiritual Prescriptions for Turbulent Times

Spiritual Prescriptions for Turbulent Times

7 Paths to Lead You Quickly from
Inner Turmoil to Inner Peace

Cathy Thomas, LPCC
Leslie S. Evelo, PhD

BALBOA.
PRESS
A DIVISION OF HAY HOUSE

Balboa Press books may be ordered through booksellers or by contacting:

Balboa Press
A Division of Hay House
1663 Liberty Drive
Bloomington, IN 47403
www.balboapress.com
1-(877) 407-4847

Because of the dynamic nature of the Internet, any web addresses or links contained in this book may have changed since publication and may no longer be valid. The views expressed in this work are solely those of the author and do not necessarily reflect the views of the publisher, and the publisher hereby disclaims any responsibility for them.

The authors of this book do not dispense medical advice or prescribe the use of any technique as a form of treatment for physical, emotional, or medical problems without the advice of a physician, either directly or indirectly. The intent of the authors is only to offer information of a general nature to help you in your quest for emotional and spiritual well-being. In the event you use any of the information in this book for yourself, which is your constitutional right, the authors and the publisher assume no responsibility for your actions.

Printed in the United States of America

ISBN: 978-1-4525-6652-8 (sc)
ISBN: 978-1-4525-6653-5 (e)
ISBN: 978-1-4525-6654-2 (hc)

Library of Congress Control Number: 2013900152

First Printing 2013
17 16 15 14 13 1 2 3 4 5

Balboa Press rev. date: 02/18/13

Dedication

This book is dedicated to our life partners, Kit and Jill, and to our wonderful friends, who have believed in us, encouraged us, and reminded us of why we were writing this book. This book was inspired by our clients and colleagues, whose amazing stories show us our own power to heal ourselves and one another.

Saint Francis of Assisi Prayer

Lord, let me be an instrument of thy peace
Where there is hatred, let me sow love;
Where there is injury, pardon;
Where there is doubt, faith;
Where there is despair, hope;
Where there is darkness, light;
Where there is sadness, joy.
O divine Master, grant that I may not so much seek
To be consoled as to console,
To be understood as to understand,
To be loved as to love;
For it is in giving that we receive;
It is in pardoning that we are pardoned;
It is in dying to self that we are born to eternal life.

Contents

PART TWO The Spiritual Prescriptions

Acknowledgements

THIS BOOK COULD NOT have been created without the help of the following people, to whom we wish to express our gratitude:

To Pam Gallagher, for encouraging Cathy to write this book, and for convincing her that she could do it. Special thanks to Janet Bray Attwood, Chris Attwood, Marci Shimoff, and Geoff Affleck for leading the weekend workshop that propelled this book into manifestation, and to Lindsay de Swart, Deb Selway, and Jim Claussen, who provided ongoing support.

To our colleagues, many of whom were willing to talk about non-traditional healing long before it was acceptable to do so. And to the therapists, clients, and friends who generously offered the stories that appear throughout this book. Their stories brought this book to life.

To Brian Weiss, MD, we are forever indebted for his courage in writing *Many Lives, Many Masters.* In doing so, he opened the door and added legitimacy to the idea that our past and "in-between" lives can offer much to the healing process.

Our deepest thanks goes to our editor, Jennifer Read Hawthorne, who took all the fear out of the editing process and instead made it positive and encouraging. Many thanks also to Adriane Pontecorvo from Balboa Publishing, who led us through the twists and turns of the publishing process and who showed an uncanny knack for getting in touch right when we needed her help.

We could not have completed this book without the unwavering support of our friends, whose faith in us kept us going when the going got tough.

We owe our most profound gratitude to our life partners, Kit and Jill, whose love, strength, and endless support made it all possible.

Introduction

HAVE YOU NOTICED LATELY that the whole world seems to be in crisis? Have your moods and emotions been bouncing all over the place for no reason? We understand! You are not alone in this experience, and we want to help you through it. That's why we've written *Spiritual Prescriptions for Turbulent Times*—as a gesture of love, to help you with the intense and overwhelming emotions you may be feeling at this time.

In our own search for tools to help us through the turmoil of our time, it occurred to us that it would be great if all of these resources could be found in one place. So we pulled together the best of these resources and created a guidebook to help you make your way more easily. It's like a toolbox of healing methods, to give you instant access to the tools you need, when you need them. We've included what we've found to be the most helpful, effective, and immediate techniques to help anyone who's hurting or in crisis to feel better quickly.

The resources, books, CDs, and websites in this book are the best ones out there, in our opinion. Choose the ones you feel drawn to; that's your intuition speaking, and it won't steer you wrong. As we come across additional resources we like, we will list them on our website, www.spiritualprescriptions.com.

WHY WE WROTE THIS BOOK

CATHY IS A PSYCHOTHERAPIST with more than twenty-five years' experience, much of it working with trauma survivors. For the first ten years of her career, she offered traditional "talk" therapy. This method was successful in many cases, but sometimes she found that her clients' issues continued to trouble them despite her best efforts.

Searching for new ways to help her clients heal, she learned about Eye Movement Desensitization and Reprocessing (EMDR). She started using it with clients, and discovered that it offered lasting recovery from trauma. She specialized in EMDR for fifteen years, and also continued to explore new developments in healing.

Along the way, Cathy became intrigued by quantum physics. The laws of quantum physics brought her a whole new understanding about how the Universe works. The connection between all living beings, non-living things, and our planet was undeniable. This changed her perceptions of just about everything—including psychotherapy and the therapy relationship—and made her want to do therapy very differently.

Cathy's exploration of spirituality and non-traditional healing was at the same time expanding her perspective of healing, and she came to understand the benefits of including non-traditional healing methods in the psychotherapy process. It was an intense period of personal and professional transformation—one that ultimately led to the writing of this book.

As her ideas about healing and her approach to psychotherapy evolved, she felt compelled to share with her clients what she was learning. She was pleasantly surprised to find that many of them were open to learning and trying new ways of healing. Their shared experiences changed and enriched Cathy's life and the lives of her clients.

Then Cathy met Leslie at a psychotherapy training seminar. Like Cathy, Leslie was a psychologist who had been working primarily in the area of trauma recovery and had arrived at a similar point of frustration with traditional psychotherapy. Many of her clients, though improved or improving, were not getting better with regard to chronic anxiety, depression, and chronic pain. Leslie had also been learning about non-traditional healing, quantum physics, and spirituality, and had begun to implement them in her psychotherapy practice.

For both of them, it was like finding a kindred spirit, and they began a rich conversation about psychotherapy, healing, and personal transformation that continues to this day. Having already begun to write this book, Cathy invited Leslie to be her co-author because, it turned out, Leslie had been feeling the same desire to share a new paradigm of transformation and healing.

Leslie and Cathy share the belief that their journeys intersected at that time through Divine grace. In *Spiritual Prescriptions for Turbulent Times* the two bring their combined fifty years of experience in working with trauma and difficult feelings—along with their extensive exploration and study of alternative and spiritual healing methods and techniques—to help anyone in crisis quickly and effectively.

Keeping an Open Mind

Some of the stories in this book arise from our own experiences with non-traditional healing. They reflect our personal views, and we do not claim them to be universally applicable. Additionally, we have included theories and methods of healing that have not been formally researched. A lot of what we talk about in this book is outside the frame of linear thinking, and may not fit with traditional paradigms.

So it may require a huge leap of faith to consider the ideas presented, and all we ask of you is that you keep an open mind as you read. Please take with you that which evokes your curiosity and interest, and leave the rest. We have attempted to provide enough resources for you to explore these ideas and their underlying research at your own pace.

It is important for us to note here that in no way do we mean to imply that psychotherapy is not a viable option for healing. Despite what we consider to be the inherent limitations of traditional therapy, psychotherapy remains an important part of healing for many people. The therapeutic relationship is the primary healing factor in psychotherapy; in fact, we now know that a good therapy relationship can help to build vital connections within the brain.

When we don't receive during childhood the type of loving, nurturing feedback from our caregivers that we need, our brains do not develop the connections that allow us to easily move between logical thinking and intuitive, emotional experience. We tend to become stuck on one side or the other, either living in our thoughts and out of touch with our feelings, or overly emotional and unable to use logic to help us problem solve.

In either case, our responses to life events are not balanced in a healthy way. If we have the opportunity to participate in a long-term, close relationship with someone—it could be a life partner or a dear friend or an excellent therapist—that relationship actually facilitates the building of the missing connections in the brain. Dr. Daniel J. Siegel has written several books on this subject, such as *The Mindful Therapist* (W.W. Norton & Company, 2010).

How to Use This Book

This book will show you how to move from feeling overwhelmed to feeling inner peace. Within the first few minutes of reading it, you will be able to access healing techniques that you can use right away. By the time you have finished reading it, you will have a collection of methods and techniques from which to choose. Picture yourself feeling stable, peaceful, and full of hope. That is how we want you to feel.

We have divided the book into three sections. In Part One, we show you the science behind alternative healing. Once you understand it, you will see that you can use your own power—your inner Divinity—to create the life you want.

Next, in Part Two, we give you the tools to help you use your power most effectively. We call them the Prescriptions, written to bring you peace in the midst of chaos.

In Part Three, we look at why we're here, at this time and on this planet. As you will see, it's not an accident. We serve a noble purpose, each and every one of us. We also include a chapter on therapy, to help you decide whether you might need it and to recommend the therapies and therapy tools that we think are most helpful.

If you need **immediate help** in getting your feelings of overwhelm under control, please go straight to Chapter 9 and use any of the techniques or therapies listed there. In fifteen minutes you should be feeling more centered. If you are feeling angry and resentful right now, check out Chapter 10 for ways to forgive whoever you believe has harmed you. Forgiveness can immediately reduce your distress, and that is the reason to do it.

If you are feeling anxious, you can find relief by practicing the simple meditation offered in Chapter 6. And if you need a therapist's help, please go to Chapter 13 for help with how to find a good therapist. Getting help from someone is often the best possible plan for getting yourself back into emotional regulation.

This book offers you many ways to help yourself. You will be intuitively drawn to those that are particularly suited to you and that will help you the most at the time you need them. We have tried our best to write a book that is not too heady or clinical. We do explain some concepts, but have tried to make them accessible and understandable.

Our intention was to write a book that is practical, one that offers effective tools to help you feel better faster. At different times you may need different resources, and we hope that you will keep this book as your source for the tools you need along the way. And don't forget to share it with your family and your friends when they're in need.

If you have started the book in a later chapter, at some point you may want to come back and start at the beginning. If not, that's okay. The important thing is that you use this book in a way that works best for you.

If you are a therapist reading this book, we thank you from the bottom of our hearts—for the difficult and sometimes painful work you do for the benefit of others, and for your willingness to entertain new ideas about therapy and healing.

If you are an individual in search of personal growth and awareness, we thank you for including this book in your quest. When we work to heal ourselves and others, the energy we create helps to heal the world.

And now is the time.

Part One

Emotional Healing in Turbulent Times

1

Transformation: A Change in Paradigm

One of Leslie's longtime clients called the other day in obvious distress. She had been awash in memories of her childhood abuse, repeating old patterns of self-destructive behavior, and feeling bewildered about where all of it was coming from. "I have everything I want, I'm doing work that I love, and I've been feeling happy and contented with my life—then, boom! All this stuff comes out of nowhere! I thought I was done with all of it! Why is this happening?" she cried.

Her story is not unlike others we have heard lately. People are experiencing emotional and spiritual challenges, including some they thought were long ago resolved. Childhood issues, past trauma, relationship conflicts, job stress … it's all coming up at once, out of the blue. It's like being on a roller coaster, only you can't see the climbs and drops until you're on top of them.

You may be reading this book because you've been feeling the same sort of things in your life—anxious, depressed, or both at once. You're not alone. A lot of us are feeling overwhelmed.

So where to start? In this chapter, we'll talk about what these times mean for us; how to open to transformation; specific alternative therapies, including medical intuitives, psychic interpretation, and energy healers; and how these "out-of-the-box" therapies offer a new paradigm for healing.

Turbulent Times

One of the things we find most helpful during these turbulent times is understanding that the turmoil and upheaval you're experiencing is supposed to be happening. You are exactly where you are supposed to be right now. You are going through all of this because you are an important part of the magnificent changes occurring in the world.

Sages and spiritual teachers around the world foretold long ago of this time, when humanity would reach this period of global upheaval. They predicted that the turbulence would result in a great transformation for the earth and for humanity. Some religious and spiritual traditions have understood this to mean a time of judgment and destruction, while others have foreseen liberation from all suffering.

Present-day teachers and healers say that we are going through something akin to childbirth, wherein the labor pain of our current struggles will birth a new era of peace, vibrant health, communion with the Divine, and connection with the earth and with all life.

Then what are we supposed to *do* with all of this turmoil? Well, it is a bit like infection rising to the top of a wound or a boil. The turmoil, like the white cells of an infection, is rising to the surface so that it can be cleansed from our wounded lives. We have to rid ourselves of all the negativity that weighs us down before we can ascend to the new, higher level of existence that will be the new era.

You have probably noticed that the earth, too, is purging herself of negativity. Earthquakes, floods, wildfires, tsunamis, tornadoes … our earth is clearing the damage that humanity has caused through reckless depletion and contamination of her natural resources. She is reminding us that she, too, is a living organism that must be nurtured in order for her—and us—to survive. The earth is restoring herself in preparation to live in harmony and connection with us and with all life that she supports.

You may doubt that you have a place in all this. You may be feeling scared, powerless, and a bit uneasy with all this "woo-woo" stuff. You may also be wondering if we are crazy!

Fair enough. However, if you are willing to keep an open mind as you read this book, we will help you to understand your vital role in this global transformation. We will share with you the healing techniques that will empower you to free yourself of the negativity in your life. And we will help you discover the wisdom and power that is already within you. Your inner wisdom and power will enable you to create the life that you truly want to live.

You were meant to be here, right here, right now. Your most important job is to heal yourself. We want to help you do that. And as you heal yourself, you also heal the world.

Transformation: A Change in Paradigm

Transformation occurs in life when you encounter situations that broaden your awareness or deepen your understanding. A major life event can shake you to your core, turn your world upside down in such a way that you are forever changed. Or something small and seemingly insignificant can shift your perception and cause you to see the world differently. Transformation can be uncomfortable or even painful, or it can be liberating and joyful. In all cases, transformation is a powerful catalyst for growth.

In the book *Living Deeply: The Art and Science of Transformation in Everyday Life,* Marilyn Mandala Schlitz and her colleagues explore the subject of transformation in depth. They write:

> Not all transformative paths start with a dramatic peak experience, but most begin with some kind of noetic experience or deeply felt, unshakable internal realization. This shift can be triggered by something as subtle as reading a book that discusses an idea new to you or by something as dramatic as a near-death experience or a sudden awareness of a physical or perceptual phenomenon that is completely unexplainable in your current belief system. Typically, these moments are characterized by recognition of some undeniable truth that flies in the face of—or puts the lie to—some fundamental belief you've held, possibly without even knowing it. (p. 203)

Several years ago, Cathy had an experience like this. She was ill with a fever that would not go away. It stuck with her for over eight months, and no one in the medical world was able to find the cause or stop the fever. At the urging of a friend, she sought the aid of Dr. David Dammert, a chiropractic healer who offers non-traditional treatments for physical and emotional issues. Cathy was quite skeptical, and doubted his ability to help her. Much to her surprise, however, her symptoms disappeared after only one treatment session, and they did not return.

Dr. Dammert used chiropractic kinesiology, a diagnostic technique that employs muscle testing. We will explore muscle testing in another chapter; for now, suffice it to say that Cathy knew nothing about this or any of the energy techniques that he utilized. But despite her initial skepticism, she felt a deep, inner knowing that she was healed. This was a transformational experience for Cathy, because if this healing was real, then many things she had previously believed could not be true.

Our limited human minds do not readily accept things that defy logic. Instead, we tend to dismiss them as misperceptions, coincidences, or random accidents. But if we suspend our disbelief, even for a moment, we are able to discern within us a deeper and more profound wisdom. It was this wisdom that allowed Cathy to know that she was healed, despite her rational mind telling her that it could not be true. She stuck with her intuition to trust Dr. Dammert's healing methods, and it proved to be a wise decision. She even convinced several of her friends, including Leslie, to see him, and they have achieved positive results as well.

You have your own internal wisdom. It's there when you get a "gut" feeling that you should or should not do something, or when you get a sense that something is true even though it does not seem possible. Interestingly, your gut feeling, or intuition, is a more reliable source of knowledge than your rational mind. If you think about this, you will undoubtedly recognize at least one instance in which your gut told you to do or to not do something, while your rational mind tried to talk you out of what your gut was telling you. Which one turned out to be correct?

There are so many situations in life that require us to challenge our limited, logical thinking. Traditional forms of treatment, such as Western medicine and "talk" therapy, are problem focused and designed to treat symptoms rather than causes. They rely upon objective, scientific data that are measurable and observable.

Eastern medicine and non-traditional forms of healing, however, focus on the causes of our maladies and problems, and look to the whole person—body, mind, and spirit—to determine appropriate treatment. Many of these healing methods use principles of energy within the body and mind, and derive their benefits from correcting or re-directing the flow of energy within and around someone in order to heal them.

Our work with Dave Dammert taught both of us about the profound connections between our physical bodies, our emotions, our minds, and our spirit. It challenged our long-held beliefs about illness and healing. We, like you, had not been taught to view the mind and body as a single system, and did not yet know that imbalance in one part of the system could cause problems in the other. But what we learned was that when mind and body are aligned, physical and mental health naturally emerge.

Traditional healing methods allow us to be passive recipients of externally derived "fixes." We take a pill and wait for it to cure us, or we get a vaccination and expect it to prevent illness. We are not required to do anything to help ourselves, other than to swallow the pills or take the shots. Non-traditional, mind/body/spirit forms of healing require us to take responsibility for at least part of our treatment and healing. We will talk much more about this in another chapter.

But the biggest thing that true healing requires is the willingness to open our minds and our bodies to treatments and techniques that utilize energy, spirit, and Divine or Universal wisdom to help us. We have to go beyond our reliance on the measurable and the observable, and accept that the Universe operates in ways that far exceed the abilities of our finite, human minds.

As the two of us experienced the power of non-traditional methods of healing, we started to explore other alternative sources of knowledge and healing. We found out more about energy healing, learned about medical intuiting, and became interested in psychic interpretation.

Medical Intuitives

Medical intuitives are individuals who possess the ability to accurately and intuitively perceive what is out of balance or *dis*-eased within the body. Kate, a former client of Leslie's, tells the following story about her consultation with a medical intuitive:

> I had been experiencing this relentless fatigue for at least four months, and it was driving me nuts. It seemed that I couldn't do the simplest thing, like walking up a flight of stairs, without stopping to rest and catch my breath. That was the other thing—I had been short of breath a lot. I saw my regular doctor, who tested me for mononucleosis, low thyroid function, anemia, lupus ... all of the tests were negative. He even sent me to an oncologist to see if I might have cancer or leukemia! That, too, was negative. I started to think that maybe I was making it all up, and that my symptoms were not real.
>
> Leslie suggested that I see a medical intuitive, which I thought was pretty weird, but I really wanted to know what was going on, so I decided to try it. When this woman met with me, she spent a few minutes looking at me to see if she could see any "visible" signs of what was wrong. She also held her hands just above my body and moved them up and down my entire body. Sometimes she held her hands up higher or farther away from areas of my body; other times her hands just hovered an inch or so above me. Then she closed her eyes and seemed to be meditating or praying, or maybe waiting for information to come to her.
>
> When she was through, she turned on the lights in the room and sat down with me to tell me what she found. She said there was a problem with a valve in my heart, that it was not functioning properly, and that it had been getting progressively worse for a while. She also said that I needed to see a heart specialist to have it checked out as soon as possible.

I had a hard time convincing my regular doctor to give me a referral, but eventually he agreed to refer me to a cardiologist. Sure enough, he ended up finding a serious problem with one of my valves, and he recommended a valve replacement. I had the surgery and it took a few months to recover completely, but now I am back to my full energy level. The shortness of breath is gone, and I really feel good. For something I was so skeptical about, this medical intuitive turned out to be right on. I credit her with saving my life!"

Psychic Interpretation

If you watch TV, read newspapers or magazines, or listen to the radio, chances are that you have heard something about psychics. People with psychic abilities are able to "see," "hear," predict, or somehow know things that are beyond our regular capacity to know. Sometimes this includes information about one's physical or emotional problems; often, it also provides information about the circumstances under which a medical, emotional, or spiritual issue has developed, and its meaning in the person's life. This information is often very helpful in understanding and healing one's problems.

Psychics have been gaining more acceptance and credibility during the past several years. They have been the subjects of popular television programs, and their skills have been utilized by law enforcement agencies for help in solving criminal investigations. It is not uncommon for people to consult with psychics in order to understand issues and challenges in their lives, or for help in communicating with loved ones who have died.

Energy Healing

Energy healing comes in different forms. Energy healers transmit energy through their hands through practices such as Reiki. Reiki practitioners serve as conduits for *chi*, universal life force energy, to be directed to the recipient for healing. Reiki wisdom is that every person's body, mind, and spirit knows what to do with *chi* when it is received, and that the energy is thus utilized in whatever ways that person most needs it. Some teachers of energy healing believe that Reiki and other energy techniques were actually the tools used by Jesus and other religious figures to perform the miraculous healings recorded in the Bible and in other religious texts.

Energy healers are becoming increasingly accepted by mainstream medicine. Hospitals often employ energy practitioners, often Healing Touch certified, as an adjunct to traditional medical treatment. Hospices invite volunteer Reiki healers to give Reiki to patients, their loved ones, and to the doctors and nurses who work with hospice patients. Its calming and soothing effects offer a welcome reprieve from the emotional and physical stresses that accompany serious or terminal illness for patients and their caregivers. And its power to rebalance the body's energy flow has been credited with boosting the body's natural ability to fight disease.

Leslie and Cathy have both received Reiki and other energy healing treatments, and we have recommended it to many clients through the years. In fact, Leslie found it so helpful in treating her chronic musculoskeletal pain that she decided to be trained as a Reiki Master practitioner. She has used Reiki to treat chronic pain, anxiety, and even pregnancy-related discomfort. One mother-to-be reported that after a Reiki session, her intense back pain was relieved when her baby actually shifted in the womb to assume a more comfortable position.

You don't have to believe that energy healing, medical intuition, or psychic interpretation is real, or that it works, in order for it to work. It does help to be open to accepting the *possibility* that it could work. But either way, it's like gravity: you don't have to believe in it in order for it to work. If you let go of something you are holding in your hand, it will fall to the ground, whether you believe that it will or not.

Our good friend Mikki Fogg shared with us the following story of her energy healing:

> First off, let me tell you that I grew up in an *extremely* logical, intellectual, and scientific home—we never spoke of spiritual things (not even God), and my entire family firmly believed that if you couldn't see, hear, touch, taste, smell, or somehow measure

something, it just plain didn't exist! And anyone who *did* believe in such nonsense was definitely a bit on the wacky side . . .

I continued this early training by following a scientific path myself—deepening my beliefs in the concreteness of the physical world by studying engineering at a renowned scientific institution: MIT. At that point in my life, I *knew* that our world was very solid and tangible, and it was all easily explained by a set of physical laws (based on Newtonian physics) that were as inescapable as gravity.

When I was in my early forties, however, I had my first experience of truly feeling energy move ... I was at a weekend retreat where we were attempting to connect more deeply with the joy inside of us (a sneaky way to get a non-believer like me to come to a "spiritual" retreat, huh?). In one exercise, four of us stood in a circle and each focused our attention on the eyes and the heart of the person across from us. Continuing this practice, the four of us then did an hour-long open-eyed meditation together.

About twenty minutes into the meditation, I began to feel a strange tingling sensation in the palms of my hands. With each in-breath, the tingling increased. Pretty soon, I could feel the energy swirling from me to the person on my left, to the person across from me, to the person on my right, and then back through me. And with each cycle, it grew stronger. I knew the others felt it also, because soon we were all swaying in unison in the direction the energy was flowing. My body was electrified, and I could feel myself melding with my three meditation partners. By now the energy was so intense that we were all beaming with broad gleeful smiles. Perhaps everything in the world was not solid and tangible after all!

Then one Sunday morning several years later, I awoke with a stabbing pain in my lower back that was so intense I couldn't get out of bed by myself. My sons were at their father's house, so I struggled to figure out what to do. Finally, I called a close friend who lived nearby, and she insisted on taking me to the emergency room at the local hospital.

As I lay in the hospital bed in one of the treatment rooms of the ER, the doctors and nurses worked over me with care and concern. One by one, they ruled out possible causes for my intense pain—no, not a kidney stone ... no, not a kidney infection ... no, not a potentially deadly pulmonary thrombosis ... After four hours and $3000+ of tests (including a CAT scan, some X-rays, and some blood work), they couldn't find the cause of my pain, so they told me it must just be due to muscle spasms. They gave me two prescriptions—one for pain and one to relax my muscles—and sent me home.

Inside, I *knew* that my pain was *not* caused by muscle spasms, so I never even filled the two prescriptions. I simply toughed it out by taking some Tylenol and trying to get some sleep. I tossed and turned all night in pain, and by the next morning, it was not any better (but now at least, my sons were home and able to bring me the things I needed so that I could stay in bed.)

That morning, by "coincidence," I had a call scheduled with an energy healer I had occasionally worked with over the phone. (Yes, I who grew up with such strong beliefs against such things, had stretched far enough that I was now occasionally working with an energy healer, AND she was doing her work remotely, over the telephone!)

When I got on the call with Gloria, she immediately asked what was going on with my back. I described my stabbing pain, and I shared about my little escapade at the ER the previous day. She stopped me short and said, "Well, we can work on that now, if you want to." I told her that of course I wanted to.

She told me to send a grounding cord to the center of the earth, and, as I did, she noticed my ex-husband's energy around me. She asked me to take any mental images I got of him and put them out in front of me and dissolve them. As I did this, the pain began to travel around the sides of my body and ultimately moved all the way to the front portion of my abdomen. It was still quite a strong pain, but now in a totally different place.

Next, Gloria asked if it would be okay if she got silent for a minute or so and "worked" on me energetically. I agreed quickly, as I was still in awe of how the pain had moved. Within that next minute, while Gloria was silently working on me, that pain completely went away—and it has never come back again!

The $75 I spent on that call with Gloria that day was some of the best money I have ever spent. I jokingly asked her what she would charge for a middle-of-the-night emergency call, compared to the $3000+ I had spent at the ER, and she said, 'If you need to call me, please call.' Wow. I'm a believer—energy work certainly *is* powerful.

Psychotherapy Re-examined

As you might imagine, psychotherapists are not trained to use alternative healing or alternative healers as a part of their work. We are taught to rely on traditional methods of using verbal language and rational thinking to conceptualize and treat client problems. We decided to include alternative healing in our therapy practices because both of us had benefitted from it ourselves, as had other people whose feedback and opinions we trusted. Clients who tried alternative treatment techniques found them quite helpful, which led us to consider recommending them to our therapist colleagues for use with their clients.

We were not at all certain how our suggestions would be received by these colleagues, but felt that the potential benefit to their clients made it worth sharing the information. Happily, we discovered that quite a few of our colleagues were already recommending alternative healing to their clients, and that they, too, were achieving positive results. We asked several of these therapists to share their experiences—and those of willing clients—with us, and have included some of their stories in this book.

Apparently, we were not alone in our emerging awareness that traditional therapy often did not address the whole person—mind, body, and spirit. Alternative healers were showing us that healing could be accomplished more efficiently and effectively by using techniques that applied principles of energy and the laws of the Universe in ways that challenged our traditional models of therapy.

2

Divinity and Energy: Quantum Physics Made Easy

You are Divinity itself. You have within you the creative power of Divine Source, and you are using it to create your life every minute of every day. And chances are, you don't even know you're doing it.

We humans are just now discovering that the energy of the Divine is within us. Until now, we have not realized our power—essential to quickly restore emotional inner peace—nor have we understood how our power works. So every day, we bring into existence a world of experiences for ourselves that usually do not match what we wish we had created.

So how can we use our power to create what we *do* want? We do so by learning how to use *energy*. Energy is the tool with which we create our lives. It is also the key to healing the emotional pain and turmoil we feel in these turbulent times.

In order to use the creative and healing power of our energy, we need to understand how it works. We'll explain the fundamental concepts of energy in this chapter, and we'll talk some more about the innate Divinity that enables us to use our energy to heal.

To understand how energy works, you need to learn a little bit of quantum physics. Now, we realize that some of you may feel squeamish at the mention of quantum physics, or fear that it will be too complex for you to grasp. Fear not, for the concepts we discuss are surprisingly easy to understand.

They are also truly amazing: they explain why alternative healing is possible. Once you understand some of quantum physics' basic principles, you will see why alternative healing is not as far-fetched as you may have thought—and why it may be the most effective way to heal.

Our Innate Divinity

There is a spark of Divinity within each one of us. We were all created by Divinity (you may call this God, Allah, Christ, or the great organizing force of the Universe), and we are made up of Divine energy. Imagine, as Wayne Dyer suggests in *Wishes Fulfilled: Mastering the Art of Manifesting*, that the ocean is the body of God, and that each of us is a cup of the ocean. We forget that we are part of the ocean, until one day we come to the ocean and say, "Oh, that's what I am. I am a part of the ocean!"

We are able to experience the Divine Source within us, and the Divine is able to experience this world through us. We are the physical manifestations of the supreme intelligence in the Universe. In the words of Fr. Pierre Teilhard de Chardin, "We are spiritual beings having a human experience" (*The Phenomenon of Man*, p. 32).

According to Eric Butterworth in *Discover the Power within You*, "... the Divinity of Man has been the best kept secret of the ages" (p. xv). It is time now for us to awaken to our inner Divinity and to learn the ways in which this world actually works.

We Are All Energy

One of the things that keeps us stuck in feeling overwhelmed and unhappy is that we believe that things in our world are solid, fixed, and unchangeable. Like our friend Mikki, whose story you read in the last chapter, we see ourselves as solid entities, separate from every other person and creature and object in the world. We see objects and structures as solid, too. And we sometimes think that our beliefs and feelings are fixed.

The truth, however, is that we humans are not solid entities at all, and neither are the creatures and objects that surround us. We are all completely made up of energy, and so is every other thing in the Universe that has form. "Solid" things are not solid; things are not as they appear. Things that we think are solid and unchanging—such as our bodies—are not. They are energy, and energy is always moving and changing. Nothing is "fixed," and everything is changeable.

Bruce Lipton, PhD, illustrates this fact in his book *The Biology of Belief.* He states: "Here you are holding this physical book in your hands. Yet if you were to focus on the book's material substance with an atomic microscope, you would see that you are holding nothing... the quantum Universe is mind-bending" (p. 101).

Everything that we are able to see or touch is actually made of particles of energy. These particles have grouped together to form the materials (wood, iron, clay, etc.) that make up the various objects in our environment. They have also grouped together to form us humans, and all other living beings and inanimate objects. At the core of us, we are the same as every other being or object in the Universe—moving particles of energy.

It is by using our energy effectively that we are able to make changes in our lives and in the world. Not only are we and everything else composed of energy, but energy is our main tool for healing. Since it is the central part of healing and changing, it's important to understand the nature of energy itself.

The first thing to know is that energy exists in two forms: waves and particles. Waves can change into particles of energy, but this is only possible under one condition: the energy must be observed.

Unbelievable as it seems, it is true. The mere act of observing energy causes it to form a particle of matter. This phenomenon is known as the Observer Effect. It's a mind-boggling fact, and one of the most mysterious and wondrous rules of quantum physics.

Particles are constantly moving, vibrating at a certain rate, or frequency. The objects they form vibrate at different frequencies: your energy vibration is faster than that of the chair you are sitting on, and its vibration is slower than your dog's vibration. Rocks are vibrating much slower than light rays, which vibrate much faster than flowers.

But how does a particle "know" what physical form it should take—whether it should take on the form of wood or grass or stone or human? As we have explained, energy changes from wave to particle when it is observed. And at that moment, it is the *observer* who chooses what physical form the particles will take! That particle of energy has the inherent potential to take the form of any conceivable thing, but it takes on whatever form is in the mind or consciousness of the person who observes it, says Lynne McTaggart in her book *The Field*. In essence, *we are creating everything we see.*

Beyond the things in our world that we can see, there is a great deal that we cannot see. It appears to us as empty space but is really a field of vibrating energy. And since we and all other things are also vibrating energy, there are no real "edges" that determine where you stop and your chair begins, or between you and another person. All of it is energy, and there is no real separation between us and anything or anyone else.

The implications of this are astounding. It means that we are connected to each other and to all that is. Our notions of "us" and "them," of separate entities, are mere illusions. We are all one, woven together to form an infinite, interconnected web. This interconnectedness forms the basis of spiritual teachings from virtually every tradition. Native American spirituality views all life—the earth, sky, water, air, moon, stars, gods, and spirits—as interwoven. Most indigenous populations throughout the world hold similar beliefs.

In Buddhism, the saying that "Form is emptiness, emptiness is form" refers to the lack of separation between things. Christianity refers to loving one's neighbor as oneself, and other religions teach similar concepts. It all comes down to the fact that there is no real difference between us. Everything is energy and it is all connected.

Thought is Energy, and Thought Affects Energy

In order to learn how we can use our energy to change and to create our own lives, it is important to understand the next fundamental concept about energy, which is that it can be affected by thought. In her book *The Field,* investigative journalist Lynne McTaggart discusses a series of scientific studies in which this premise was investigated in a way that they could visibly observe it.

The scientists behind these studies, Princeton University's Dr. Robert Jahn and his colleague Dr. Brenda Dunne, designed and conducted experiments to determine whether thoughts could change the function of machines. They utilized machines that were called Random Number

Generators (RNG's) and Random Event Generators (REG's), both of which produced random numbers or events. For example, the machine could generate a random sequence of "yes" or "no," "on" or "off," or "1" or "0" responses. It was, in essence, a mechanized version of the coin flip, where there was a 50% chance of obtaining "heads" and a 50% chance of a "tails" result.

Jahn and Dunne performed hundreds of experiments, and millions of subsequent trials were done. The scientists wanted to be certain that the results they were obtaining were consistent each time an experimental trial was conducted. In each experiment, participants were asked to try to affect the way the machines operated by intentionally focusing their thoughts on how they wanted them to operate.

Jahn and Dunne amassed mountains of data, and they managed to show with scientific precision that in every single case, the subjects were able to influence the machines in such a way that the responses generated were no longer random. Virtually every possible contaminating variable—that is, anything else that could influence the machine's responses—was eliminated, so the results could not be explained by anything other than the will of the human subjects to influence the machines in one direction or the other.

Said McTaggert, "This was as rigorous a scientific study as they come, and yet somehow their participants—all ordinary people, no psychic superstars among them—had been able to affect the random movement of machines simply by an act of will" (*The Field,* p. 115).

What Jahn and Dunne had proven, in effect, was that *thought itself is a form of energy, capable of influencing other energy* in its various forms. It was a revolutionary idea, and yet most of us have never heard of it.

Jahn and Dunne established an institute of sorts, dubbed the PEAR (Princeton Engineering Abnormalities Research) project, whose sole purpose was to scientifically study the effects of conscious thought on random phenomena. The program was active for decades, from the 1970s to 2007. The contributions of the PEAR project scientists to our understanding of the power of human thought energy cannot be underestimated. They provided the scientific rigor necessary to validate what had previously been dismissed as folly.

Most of us have influenced the operation of a machine without even knowing it. Case in point: have you ever tried to use your computer at a time when you were feeling emotionally upset? If so, you may have discovered that it would not boot up, or the mouse would not work, or that it would not respond to your keystrokes. Perhaps you grew even more upset, yelled at the thing, got up, and stomped away in frustration. Later, when you were calmer, you may have returned to your computer and found, much to your surprise, that it was once again working.

What had caused it to stop working in the first place? Most likely, the intense emotional energy within and surrounding you had disrupted the computer's electrical system. Once your energy calmed, the circuits were no longer disrupted and the computer's normal functioning was restored.

Powerful energy healers and psychics sometimes report that audio, electrical equipment, and lightbulbs tend to stop working in their presence. Wristwatches often do not work for them either. Their energy simply overwhelms the electrical energy of the systems around them. A psychic with whom Leslie consults once told her that when she (the psychic) experiences large influxes of psychic information, it's not uncommon for all the lightbulbs in her house to blow out in one day, or for both her television and computer to stop working. These incidents serve as tangible evidence of the power of our energy to influence our environment.

One of the most beautiful and powerful examples of the dramatic influence of our energy upon all that surrounds us is the work of Dr. Masaru Emoto, whose photographs have had a profound effect on millions of people across the world. Dr. Emoto sought to demonstrate the impact of thought energy expressed through words, and he wanted to do so in a way that we could actually observe with our eyes.

Dr. Emoto studied the effects of various forms of energy upon water by photographing the ice crystals from water samples that were frozen after being exposed to spoken words, written words, music, and photographs. What are words, after all? They are thoughts expressed in language, which humans invented long ago in order to communicate thoughts to one another. Since thoughts are a form of energy, so must be the words that communicate those thoughts.

In his experiments, Dr. Emoto compared the effects of positive words and negative words on water. The positive words included "Love and Gratitude," "You're beautiful," "Wisdom," and "Cosmos." The negative words were: "You fool!," "You make me sick. I want to kill you!" and "Satan." These words were either spoken to the water or written on pieces of paper and wrapped around the water containers, so that the words faced the water.

The water was then frozen and photographs were taken of the ice crystals that formed in the water. What Dr. Emoto found was amazing: the crystals formed in water that had received positive words were beautiful with intricate designs, and they carried lovely energy to those who viewed them. In contrast, the water exposed to negative words produced malformed, ugly crystals, whose energy felt dark and very unpleasant. The effects were the same whether the messages were written or spoken.

"Love and Gratitude"

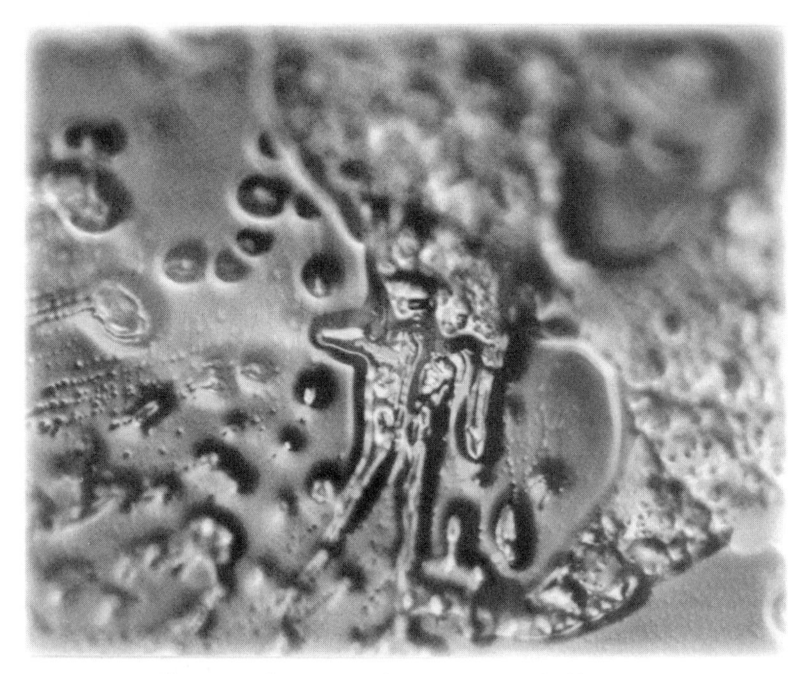

"You make me sick. I want to kill you."

He also exposed water to classical music, prayer chants, and heavy metal music with violent lyrics. As you might expect, the classical music and chants created beautiful crystals, while those formed in response to the violent heavy metal music were fragmented and disorganized.

Perhaps the most surprising and awe-inspiring experiments were those that were done with water that had been "shown" photographs—of Earth, a crop circle, a goddess, and a dolphin. This water formed exquisite crystals, and the energy they carried was quite powerful.

Leslie shared the following story after she saw the one photo in particular:

> I have always felt a deep and powerful connection to dolphins and whales. I could never explain it, but their effect on me has been something I have felt to my core for as long as I can remember. When I saw the photo of ice crystals from water exposed to a picture of a dolphin … I can hardly explain it. I felt it in my chest—right around my heart chakra—a pounding

vibration and movement that extended upward to my throat ... it felt like my heart was opening and just surging with energy. And then this sense of incredible peace came over me, and a sort of knowing or wisdom that that connection was there for a reason and that all was well.

Dolphin

Others who have seen Dr. Emoto's photographs report similar experiences from viewing them. The crystals seem to vibrate with healing energy! The photos of the crystals carry this energy and transmit it to viewers. Dr. Emoto's photographs are displayed in his remarkable book *The Hidden Messages in Water* and others.

If words can change the structure of water, they can surely impact us and those to whom we speak them. Dr. Emoto urges us to be mindful of how we speak to ourselves and to others, since our words carry energy with the power to create beauty or destruction. It is also worth noting that the human body is made up of 70% water, so we know that our bodies are profoundly influenced by what we speak, see, and hear.

In addition to our capacity to affect outside objects with our thoughts, scientists have begun to recognize the power of our thoughts to influence our biology. Bruce Lipton (the cellular biologist to whom we referred earlier) has studied this extensively, and states in *The Biology of Belief* that: "Biological behavior can be controlled by invisible forces, including thought, as well as it can be controlled by physical molecules like penicillin … " (p.84).

It has long been known that thoughts affect our emotions; negative thoughts tend to produce negative emotion while positive thoughts lead to positive emotions. The psychotherapy model of Cognitive Behavioral Therapy (CBT) is based upon this thought/feeling connection. The basic premise of all the variations of CBT is that you can change your emotions and moods by changing your thought habits.

Author Louise Hay was one of the first popular healers who taught that the same sort of connection existed between thoughts, emotions, and physical healing. Her now famous book on the subject, *You Can Heal Your Life*, explored the use of self-affirmations (positive statements written in the present tense) to heal the physical body. She has been able to pinpoint which emotional issues lead to which particular ailments, and her book offers specific affirmations to remedy each illness.

Hay had been a Science of Mind practitioner and healer. Science of Mind is a spiritual philosophy that teaches that the secret to living a successful life is to consciously choose positive and productive thoughts. (*Science of Mind Magazine*, website, http://www.scienceofmind.com). She began to notice that certain emotional issues and thought patterns were often linked with specific physical ailments. She kept detailed notes of these observations over time, and witnessed over and over again the same connections between mental habits and physical problems.

For example, she noticed that throat complaints were often connected with a person's need to "speak up," to give voice to their needs, opinions, and feelings. To resolve their throat issue, the person would need to change their thinking (i.e., from "I should not speak my feelings" to "I have the right to speak my feelings"), then change their behavior by voicing their feelings. According to Hay, the person's physical throat issues would then resolve naturally. She compiled her ideas into a book to help others learn to heal themselves. Her work also discussed the importance of raising one's own vibration by learning to love and to forgive oneself.

Based upon all of the ideas, research, and information we have discussed, one thing is clear: thoughts are energy, and they have very real effects on the machines, water, objects, people, and energy that surround them. Our thoughts are powerful creative tools that we can use to heal our lives and our world.

The Laws of Attraction and Manifestation

Another fundamental concept from quantum physics that can help us shift out of our unhappiness is the Law of Attraction. This metaphysical law states that you create and attract to you what you focus your attention on. In the book *Ask and It Is Given,* Esther and Jerry Hicks state: "Every thought vibrates, every thought radiates a signal, and every thought attracts a matching signal back … " (p. 25).

Simply stated, what you think about is what you create, or "like attracts like." If you focus on the present unhappiness of your life, your energy will follow those thoughts and you will create more experiences that hold that energy. If instead you focus on what you want, and feel the excitement of how it will be to have what you want, you cause a positive change in the vibration of the energy. This will draw to you more of the positive experiences that you desire.

Consider where you actually are in your life and practice imagining what you would truly love to have for yourself in the future. This is the way to create a life in which you will thrive, instead of one in which you merely exist and feel less than happy. Try playing this simple game, which we adapted from *Ask And It Is Given* (p. 47): Complete the question, "*Wouldn't it be fun if* ________________ *?*" filling the blank with something that you would love to bring about for yourself and your life. Repeat the exercise over and over, until you have exhausted your imagination for the time being.

For example:
"*Wouldn't it be fun if*__________________ :

- we had a million dollars, and could take a three-month trip around the world?
- we could quit our jobs and retire in St. Kitts?
- we could cure world hunger?

You get the idea. Have some fun. If you play this little game with a group of friends, you can build upon each other's ideas and develop wonderful visions for all of your lives! And you'll raise your emotional frequency.

The value in an exercise like this one is that it gives you permission to put your dreams out there, no matter how "impossible" they may seem. Our society as a whole is so focused on negative energy that we have come to mistake it for reality. We labor under the assumption that "this is just the way things are" and wrongly believe that there is nothing we can do about our life circumstances.

But as we have just been discussing, there is something you can do! You can embrace the creative power of your thoughts—focus your energy on what you want and practice that positive focus again and again. Thoughts are energy and they affect energy. Make a habit of noticing when you are thinking negatively, and immediately switch your thinking to positive thoughts and dreams. For example, if you notice yourself thinking, "I don't have enough money to do the things that make me happy," intentionally switch that thought to, "I have all the money I could possibly want, and more!" If you do this every time you find yourself dwelling in the negative, you will create a cascade of positive energy in your body, mind, and spirit.

The following quote from *Discover the Power Within You* sums the whole idea up quite nicely: "You may not like what your consciousness has drawn to you. You may not like what you see in your world, but it is your attitudes and reactions that have been the attracting force. You can change the pattern of attraction and change your world" (p. 66).

You may be surprised to know that these ideas about our power to attract and manifest are not new. Quantum physics is not new. Einstein and other brilliant scientists contemplated the mysteries of quantum physics long ago. In the early 1900s, Florence Scovel Shinn wrote an affirmation about attracting abundance and our "Divine Right." Perhaps she was referring to that spark of Divinity within us all that allows us to manifest our dreams: "Infinite Spirit, open the way for my great abundance. I am an irresistible magnet for all that belongs to me by Divine Right" (*The Writings of Florence Scovel Shinn*, p.8).

A few years ago, we discovered Mike Dooley's *Notes From the Universe,* through which he sends daily email messages to remind people that they can change their lives by changing their focus. His messages are joyful and encouraging. In one recent email, he wrote:

> Tell me, when you think of taking consistent action in the general direction of your dreams, Cathy, do you imagine discipline, stamina, work, sacrifice, monotony, courage and strategies, or are you thinking adventure, discovery, new friends, excitement at the crack of dawn, magic, surprises, fun, laughter, and on occasion, the Macarena?
>
> Cool!
> The Universe
> PS. Your chosen perspective, Cathy, changes everything.

These little reminders create an instant charge of positive energy, which is a wonderful way to begin your day. You can subscribe to receive them for free at http://www.tut.com.

Dr. Wayne Dyer, in *Wishes Fulfilled*, offers another technique to use at the end of the day, in the last few minutes before you go to sleep. He suggests that you think of a few things that you want to manifest in your life, and that you form "I AM" statements with them. For example, Leslie uses statements like these:

- "***I AM*** full of energy."
- "***I AM*** a successful author."
- "***I AM*** love."
- "***I AM*** vibrantly healthy."
- "***I AM*** joyful."

Dr. Dyer explains that when you say "I AM," you are speaking as the Divine—and therefore I AM statements are very powerful creators. He encourages the use of these positive I AM declarations just before sleep, and says that it is helpful to focus on the positive feelings that you will feel when your I AM statements become reality in your life. This primes the subconscious, so it can work toward manifesting your dreams while you sleep, without interference from your logical conscious mind.

The Law of Attraction is at the heart of the recent movie *The Secret*, with which many of you are familiar. *The Secret* features a group of people who explain how they have used the law of attraction to manifest—to create, or bring into being—the lives they most desired. They also teach how you can utilize these same principles to create what you want in your life. What you think about, talk about, feel, and do determines what you bring to yourself and to the world.

If we spend most of our time thinking negative thoughts, feeling angry or hopeless, and speaking and acting accordingly, we draw to us more negativity—negative energy, people, events, thoughts, and feelings. This is the Law of Attraction at work. Our negative energy is creating the very scenarios and events that we spend our time thinking about, because that is where our attention and focus is placed.

Instead of directing your thought, feeling, word, and action energies toward negative things that you don't want, direct your energy toward positive things that you do want. Major life transformations can and do occur when you understand and utilize the laws of attraction and manifestation.

The laws of attraction and manifestation explain, in part, why traditional psychotherapy sometimes fails us. The focus of traditional therapy has been largely upon the negative patterns or troublesome issues that occur in our lives. At times, it is also focused on the past and how it has led to present situations. According to the laws of attraction and the principle of manifestation, this negative focus creates and draws to us the very negative energy and events that we are trying to avoid! It could be that in order for psychotherapy to lead to healing, it should help clients to change their thinking in a positive direction—toward what they want to create in their lives versus maintaining their focus on negative issues.

As trauma therapists, we realize that focusing on the trauma is necessary to a certain extent. What we have come to understand, though, is that the focus on trauma should remain only until it can be cleared. This clearing can be accomplished using any or all of the energy clearing techniques that we will be presenting in Chapter 9. Once the trauma has been cleared, the focus must quickly shift to the positive changes that the client wishes to make. The shift in focus from negative to positive creates the shift in energy that allows the client to activate his or her true creative power.

You can think of it in the same way as learning a new behavior, such as riding a bike. You have to practice bike-riding behaviors—pedaling, balancing, turning, stopping—in order to master the task. Repeated practice leads to better bike riding, and soon you can do it without thinking about it. It becomes automatic. So it goes with your thoughts: you have to stop practicing the negative thoughts associated with your problems, and start practicing positive thoughts about how you want your life to be. The more you practice the positive thinking, the more automatic it becomes. You generate more positive energy within yourself. This, in turn, draws to you the positive energy and events that you are trying to cultivate.

Healing With The Masters is a wonderful resource for learning to manifest what you truly desire. Jennifer McLean, a healer and entrepreneur, hosts a regularly scheduled web series with world renowned spiritual teachers and healers, many of whom offer programs on manifesting and on using the positive energy of love and compassion to heal the world. We both listen regularly to her shows with these master teachers (people like Wayne Dyer, Sonia Choquette, Jo Dunning, Neale Donald Walsch, and Panache Desai), and both of us consider *Healing With The Masters* to be a very valuable source of healing and inspiration. You can find *Healing With The Masters* at http://www.healingwiththemasters.com.

Esther Hicks, to whom we referred earlier, is a well-known channel (one whose body can serve as a human vehicle through which teachers from the other side are able to communicate) who voices communications from a group of spiritual teachers known collectively as "Abraham." These channeled communications have been the subject of several books in which Esther and recently deceased husband Jerry Hicks share Abraham's teachings.

Chief among Abraham's teachings is that you are Divine Energy, and that you have the ability to manifest what you want in this life. As Abraham stated in *Ask and it is Given*: "Everything in your physical environment was created from Non-Physical perspective by that which you call Source. And just as Source created your world, and you, through the power of focused thought, you are continuing to create your world from your Leading Edge place in this time-space reality" (p. 16).

When you change the energy of your thoughts from negative to positive, you are actually raising the vibration of your energy to a higher level. As you do so, you raise the vibration of the energy around you, and this energy affects everyone and everything you encounter. That positive, high-vibration energy generates more positive energy, so that this wonderful energy continues to radiate outward, farther and farther. When you purposefully raise your vibrations, the positive effects reach far beyond you.

3

Energy Vibration: What Is It and What Difference Does It Make?

In this chapter we will build upon our discussion of energy and the levels at which it vibrates. We and many other healers believe that one of our purposes on earth is to raise our vibrations, which will enable us to feel happier and more at peace. This, in turn, will help us to raise the vibration of our earth and everyone on it.

In order to accomplish this, we must make use of some very effective tools. One of these tools is a vast store of Universal knowledge that contains all the information we need to know in order to change our lives and change the world. In this chapter we'll show you how to tap into that knowledge using a simple process known as muscle testing.

We'll also explore how our emotions impact us. We learned in the last chapter how our thoughts affect our energy, and now we'll show how negative emotions lower your vibration, while positive emotions offer healing by raising your vibration.

And finally, we will teach you about an amazing phenomenon known as *critical mass*—the ticket to raising the vibration of everyone and everything on earth!

The Universal Database

Wouldn't it be amazing if we could all be connected to the same, humongous database of wisdom and knowledge? If the Universe's infinite wisdom was there, waiting for us to tap into it whenever we chose? Imagine the things we could do if we had that wealth of shared knowledge! The good news is that we can do all those things, because that database *does* exist.

In the last chapter, we talked about the interconnectedness of all that is, the reality that there is no separation between us and everything else. All of it is energy, and the "empty" space between things that appear to be solid is actually a vast field of vibrating, pulsating energy. Let's look now at how that vast field of energy enables us to connect with, learn from, and teach one another.

Quantum physicists refer to this as the Zero Point Field, or, more simply, the Field. Lynne McTaggart's entire book *The Field* is about the Zero Point Field and its implications for humanity and the Universe, and we have borrowed from her work in order to explain these amazing concepts to you.

According to McTaggart, the Field is made up of energy that exists in waves, and the waves connect all "things" in the Universe to one another. These waves "spread out through time and space and can carry on to infinity, tying one part of the Universe to every other part" (*The Field*, p. 24). The waves are also carriers of information. When two waves meet and overlap each other, they exchange that information, and each wave is imprinted with every bit of information from the other wave. Waves have an infinite capacity for storing information, so as they meet up and collide with other waves, they gather up more and more information. And this process goes on constantly, extending to the farthest reaches of the Universe.

What this means is that the Field contains all the information that exists and that ever has existed. It is " … a kind of shadow of the Universe for all time, a mirror image and record of everything that ever was" (*The Field*, p. 26). There is no knowledge, no understanding that does not dwell within the Field—that "empty" space that surrounds all of us.

You are connected to the Field. Its energy overlaps and mixes with your energy, so that you are constantly taking in all the wisdom of the Universe. As new knowledge is discovered, it is added to the Field via the waves of thought energy that it generates. And in this way, we are all constantly learning from and being influenced by all that knowledge.

Whether you know it or not, you already have around you and within you all of the answers to all of the questions you could ever ask. That is not conjecture or myth; it is a matter of quantum physics.

It is the Divine within you.

Your Body Holds the Proof

How can you prove to yourself that you have all this wisdom within you? It turns out that your body can demonstrate to you that you know much more than you think you know.

The human body can signal information about things—objects, substances, people, beliefs—that are present in your surroundings or in your life. Your body can tell you whether something is true or false, good for you or not good for you, trustworthy or not trustworthy, and probably many other qualities of the things, people, and ideas in your world. This is accomplished through an extensively researched process known as muscle testing, or applied kinesiology.

Kinesiology is the study of muscles and their movements. Applied kinesiology was a term coined by scientist Dr. George Goodheart, who conducted a series of experiments to explore how muscles in the human body reacted to exposure to harmful substances versus helpful substances. When he exposed people to things that were either helpful or non-harmful, their muscles remained strong. When he exposed them to substances that were not healthy, their muscles instantly became weak. The results were the same for every person tested.

These experiments demonstrated that the body has its own intuitive wisdom. You can "ask" your body whether or not something is healthy for you by using this simple process, known as muscle testing (*Applied Kinesiology,* 12th Edition. Detroit: Privately Published, 1976).

To do muscle testing, two people are required. No scientific knowledge is needed, so anyone can do it. One person serves as the "subject" (person being tested), and the other is the "tester" (one doing the testing). The two people stand facing each other, and the subject holds one arm out to the side, parallel to the floor, elbow straight. The other arm stays relaxed at their side. The tester puts one hand on the shoulder of the subject's relaxed arm, and two fingers of their other hand just above the wrist of the subject's extended arm.

Next, some sort of substance is placed near the subject. The tester gently presses down on the subject's extended arm, using only the two fingers. If the extended arm remains parallel to the floor, it is testing "strong." The "strong" response indicates that the substance is healthy, or at least not harmful, to them. If the arm falls to the subject's side, it is testing "weak." This response means that the substance is not healthy for them.

Goodheart's most famous study used muscle testing for artificial sweetener. The artificial sweetener was placed in a white envelope so that neither the testers nor the subjects knew what the substance was. Every person tested "weak" when the envelope containing artificial sweetener was placed near them. This artificial sweetener test was repeated countless times with people all around the world, and the results were the same every time. There was an apparently universal, innate knowledge that this substance was not good for the body.

Dr. John Diamond later decided to see if muscle testing would work for positive versus negative emotions and ideas. He used statements such as "I hate you" and "I love you" in his experiments. Just as you would think, people muscles tested "strong" with positive statements and "weak" with negative ones.

Dr. David Hawkins then expanded the research by conducting experiments that used muscle testing for questions about attitudes, thoughts, feelings, situations, and relationships. He found that, just as artificial sweetener is unhealthy for us, so are certain "baser," or negative, emotions and attitudes. In his book *Power vs. Force,* he shows that in the same way, positive feelings and attitudes are healthier for us.

In their book *Ask and It Is Given,* Esther and Jerry Hicks teach that different emotions vibrate at different frequencies. Positive emotions, such as Joy, Love, Passion, Appreciation, and Optimism, all vibrate at higher levels than do negative emotions such as Anger, Hatred, Guilt, Fear, and Despair (p. 114). Their "Emotional Guidance Scale" comes directly from Abraham (the group of spirit guides whom they channel), who also tells us that: "The thing that matters most is that you consciously reach for a feeling that is improved (i.e., more positive). The word for the feeling is not important" (p. 115).

You can probably recognize this for yourself. Think about how you feel physically and emotionally when you feel guilty or ashamed. It's a heavy, leaden sort of experience. On the other hand, what is it like when you feel compassion, or when you are at peace? There's a certain lightness to it, a sense of ease.

Our higher emotions and attitudes also have the higher levels of energy vibration, and the lower states of mind have the lower vibrations. You are vibrating at a much higher level when you feel compassion than when you feel ashamed. Your state of mind affects the overall level at which you vibrate; you, in turn, affect the vibrational levels around you. It follows that when you consciously direct your thoughts and emotions toward these higher states of being, you raise your individual—and our collective—vibration.

Critical Mass and Morphic Resonance

Another important metaphysical concept to help us understand the power of our energy to effect change in our own lives and in the world is that of *critical mass.* Before we examine it, though, it will be helpful to recall our earlier discussion of the Observer Effect. This rule states that before something can be manifested into form, it must be observed by consciousness. Based upon this thinking, if millions of people come to observe the events of the world differently, they can together effect huge change. They can actually create the world in which they want to live.

Some readers may recall Oprah Winfrey's worldwide webinar based upon spiritual teacher Eckhart Tolle's book *A New Earth.* Tolle emphasizes the importance of being in the present moment, fully noticing and savoring every aspect of your experience in this particular minute. Being present involves noticing your thoughts, feelings, and physical sensations as they are. When you do this, you are able to decide whether there is some aspect of your experience—thought, feeling, or sensation—that you wish to change.

If you are thinking negative thoughts, for example, you can become aware of them and then decide if those are the thoughts you want to perpetuate. Knowing that negative thoughts create negative energy, you can choose to redirect your thoughts in a positive direction—toward what you want to manifest. Your energy is thus changed, and your vibration raised, in a positive direction. It is by this simple practice that you embrace your own Divinity and creativity.

Oprah's webinar was enormously successful, and it reached millions of people. For many, it was their first introduction to the notion of their power to create the lives they want to live, and to manifest the world in which they want to live. It offered people around the world the opportunity to collectively shift their perceptions of humanity's power and purpose on this earth. Such a major shift by so many people at once created a significant and positive change in the vibration of the entire earth.

But how, exactly, did a perceptual shift experienced by several million people change the vibration of our *entire planet*? In order to understand such an awesome phenomenon, we turn to the concept of critical mass.

In physics, *critical mass* is defined as the amount of material that must be present before a chain reaction can sustain itself (*The American Heritage® New Dictionary of Cultural Literacy, Third Edition).* Originally a concept from nuclear physics, it has taken on a broader meaning in the areas of quantum physics and sociology. For our purposes, we will first use the term as it applies to quantum physics and, in particular, our levels of vibration. We will then discuss how critical mass has the potential to strongly and positively influence humanity and the earth.

As we just discussed, when you raise your own vibration, you increase the vibration of everything and everyone around you. That higher vibration extends outward from you and continues to radiate farther and farther. At some point, the higher vibration reaches so far that something wondrous occurs. In one magical instant, the vibration of all of humanity and of the entire earth raises to that higher level. And once this occurs, it cannot be undone.

This happens because the amount of energy that is vibrating at the higher level has reached critical mass. When a certain amount of the energy within something is vibrating at a high enough frequency, the remaining energy is pulled up to the higher level. This happens with people, objects, species, countries, planets … everything!

Morphic resonance is another concept related to the levels at which energy vibrates and its effect on surrounding energy. Dr. Rupert Sheldrake discusses this concept in his book *Morphic Resonance: The Nature of Formative Causation*. When an event occurs, the energy vibrations from that event spread outward, changing the vibration of the surrounding energy, which begins to *resonate* with, or assume the same vibration of, the initial energy.

This creates a *morphic field* of energy that vibrates at that level. If the energy is negative, the surrounding energy will match its lower vibration. Likewise, positive energy will raise the vibration of the surrounding energy. That's why it is so important to make sure that the energy you put out into the world is positive! Energy that vibrates at a higher frequency—the kind that comes from love, gratitude, peace, and compassion—will raise the energy it meets and continue to spread outward.

In order to test Dr. Sheldrake's theory of morphic resonance, an English TV station did an experiment during one of their broadcasts. They designed two paintings that appeared to be random patterns, but both contained hidden images that were not visible. One contained a figure of a man with a mustache, and the other a figure of a woman wearing a hat.

Before the program aired, a group of participants was shown the paintings and then asked what they had seen. Next, during the live airing of the program, it was revealed to this group that that one of the paintings contained the hidden image of the man with the mustache. Finally, a second group of participants who had not been allowed to see or hear the program viewed the paintings and were asked what they saw.

If the phenomenon of morphic resonance held true, what would you expect to have happened? Indeed, the second group was more successful at identifying the man with the mustache. The experimenters controlled as many factors as possible so that nothing other than morphic resonance could explain the results.

Ken Keyes, Jr.'s story, entitled *The Hundredth Monkey,* is a well-known illustration of morphic resonance in action. Although it is believed that he embellished certain details of it for literary effect, it is an enjoyable tale that teaches us the important concept of the impact of our behavior—that what we put out there can change the world. The story appears below in its entirety:

> The Japanese monkey, Macaca Fuscata, had been observed in the wild for a period of over 30 years.
>
> In 1952, on the island of Koshima, scientists were providing monkeys with sweet potatoes dropped in the sand. The monkeys liked the taste of the raw sweet potatoes, but they found the dirt unpleasant
>
> An 18-month-old female named Imo found she could solve the problem by washing the potatoes in a nearby stream. She taught this trick to her mother. Her playmates also learned this new way and they taught their mothers too.
>
> This cultural innovation was gradually picked up by various monkeys before the eyes of the scientists. Between 1952 and 1958 all the young monkeys learned to wash the sandy sweet potatoes to make them more palatable. Only the adults who imitated their children learned this social improvement. Other adults kept eating the dirty sweet potatoes.
>
> Then something startling took place. In the autumn of 1958, a certain number of Koshima monkeys were washing sweet potatoes—the exact number is not known. Let us suppose that when the sun rose one morning there were 99 monkeys on Koshima Island who had learned to wash their sweet potatoes. Let's further suppose that later that morning, the hundredth monkey learned to wash potatoes.
>
> THEN IT HAPPENED!
>
> By that evening almost everyone in the tribe was washing sweet potatoes before eating them. The added energy of

> this hundredth monkey somehow created an ideological breakthrough!
>
> But notice: A most surprising thing observed by these scientists was that the habit of washing sweet potatoes then jumped over the sea ... Colonies of monkeys on other islands and the mainland troop of monkeys at Takasakiyama began washing their sweet potatoes.
>
> Thus, when a certain critical number achieves an awareness, this new awareness may be communicated from mind to mind.
>
> Although the exact number may vary, this Hundredth Monkey Phenomenon means that when only a limited number of people know of a new way, it may remain the conscious property of these people.
>
> But there is a point at which if only one more person tunes in to a new awareness, a field is strengthened so that this awareness is picked up by almost everyone!

Lynne McTaggart, to whom we referred earlier in this chapter, recognized that miraculous healing was possible and within the reach of everyone—and that science proved it. This recognition turned old beliefs about healing on their heads. As she wrote in *The Field*: "If consciousness itself created order—or indeed in some way created the world—this suggested much more capacity in the human being than was currently understood. It also suggested some revolutionary notions about humans in relation to their world and the relation between all living things" (p. 104).

McTaggart's next book, *Living the Field,* offered guidance for living in alignment with the new paradigm of healing.

It is impossible to ignore that all of the healers, writers, wisdom channels, and researchers we have discussed so far are saying the same kinds of things: that we have the innate, creative power to manifest healing and vibrational shift in our lives, and that by raising our own vibrations we raise that of the entire world.

Envision peace, compassion, safe food and water supplies, freedom from disease and from all forms of suffering, and abundant joy for yourself, the earth, and all beings. *That is the key to healing the world,* and you have the power to do it. It's a matter of quantum physics. And we believe it is your purpose for being on earth at this time.

4

Empowering Ourselves: We Are Not Victims

It is not easy to accept responsibility for our lives. It's so much easier to see ourselves as products of our pasts. Certain things have happened to us that have made us the way we are. Right?

Well, yes. And no. True, your past experiences have shaped you. But they haven't made you who you are. The things that have happened in your past are merely this: they are the bridges that have carried you to where you are now—nothing more, nothing less. They do not have the power to determine the rest of your life, unless you give them that power.

If you think of yourself solely as a victim of circumstance, you turn away from your creative power. Sometimes it feels easier to do that. But it can also leave you feeling stuck in bitterness and hopelessness. The psychology of victimhood always points backward. You spend a great deal of time thinking about the past and feeling powerless, which only serves to recreate the events of the past.

In this chapter, we'll look at ways to empower ourselves: how to use the past as teacher, how to take responsibility for our futures, how to discover our passions, and how to use the present moment to make the best choices for ourselves.

The Past as Teacher

One way we disempower ourselves is to use our pasts to define who we are. In her book *Why People Don't Heal,* Carolyn Myss discusses our tendency to identify with our issues—such as abuse, chemical dependency, and mental or physical illness. For example, if you say, "I am a sexual abuse survivor," "I am an alcoholic," or "I am depressed," you state to the world that that is who you are. The more you use the label, the more you think of yourself in that way, which generates more of that energy in your life. But you are so much more than the challenges you face!

Instead of identifying with your issues, Myss suggests that you describe yourself as you truly are—a Divine being with the power to create your own life. That is your true identity, regardless of the challenges you have faced.

Even within the confines of significant limitations, such as physical injury, handicap, disease, and limited financial resources, you still have the power to choose and to create your life. Unless your thinking process is somehow damaged, leaving you unable to comprehend abstract or complex ideas, you can direct your thought energy toward the positive things that you have and that you want in your life.

In her book *Kitchen Table Wisdom*, author Rachel Naomi Remen tells the story of an athlete who lost his leg to cancer. He reacted initially with self-pity and bitter anger toward everyone who was healthy. Over time, however, his perspective changed. Rather than considering himself an unlucky victim, he began to view himself as a vessel that had been broken so that his Divine light could more easily shine through. He decided to use his experience to help people who were facing similar circumstances.

Think for a moment about how our culture teaches us to approach illness or adversity. We use terms like "conquer" and "defeat," and we view emotional distress or physical illness as enemies that must be vanquished. The alternative, as Dawna Markova (*No Enemies Within)* suggests, is to view them as teachers that offer the gift of deeper wisdom. When something "bad" happens in your life, she says, you should ask yourself what it is here to teach you. What suffering are you creating for yourself by resisting it? Is it possible for you to trust that what is happening is in Divine order?

In the midst of struggle or unhappiness, it is helpful to look at your life from a larger perspective. In *Man's Search for Meaning*, Victor Frankl describes how, in the face of unbearable suffering, he managed to find peace when he realized that he could choose his attitude by directing the path of his thought and emotion. He survived captivity in a concentration camp by accepting his circumstances as they were and responding to them with peace and deep compassion. He embodied this state of peaceful acceptance and compassion in his interactions with others, and his presence brought comfort and healing to many prisoners.

Taking Responsibility

For over thirty years Wayne Dyer has written about personal growth and the importance of our taking responsibility for our lives as a way to move out of victimhood and into empowerment. He has shared his own journey of coming to terms with his painful past and recognizing that everything that happened in his life was for his benefit and his growth. His past was the bridge that carried him to where he was, the point at which he could take responsibility for creating the rest of his life. The past was not his doing, but the present and the future were his responsibility.

In her book *No Enemies Within: A Creative Process for Discovering What's Right about What's Wrong*, Dawna Markova underscores the importance of embracing our responsibility—and our ability—to create our futures. She writes: "A great deal of time in healing is spent on working with the traumas of the past, but relatively little is directed toward creating the possibilities of a future … We have to give our minds a horizon to reach toward. We all need a vital passion, a desire to extend, an internally-driven purpose to carry us like a tiger, or a strong wind, across the abyss we encounter at a turning point (pp. 265-266)."

Sue, a friend of Cathy's, encountered personal and financial challenges that left her feeling hopeless and in despair. Then she decided to take charge of her situation by meditating on what she wanted to create. Here is her story:

> I was starting to feel trapped. For the past ten years, I had poured my heart and soul into running a Wellness Center. Another summer was coming to an end and I was flat out exhausted. I was fed up with low reimbursement rates from insurance, struggling to manage a staff of temperamental therapists, and fearful about

not making enough money to pay the huge utility bills that coming winter. I was not having fun anymore.

On the other hand, I loved the life coaching services I was now doing, and I wanted to do more. I also wanted to retain a few therapists so I could continue to offer therapy, but without any interface with insurance companies. Would people pay for services out of pocket? I feared they wouldn't.

All of this was complicated by the fact that I owned the building that housed the Wellness Center. I had rehabbed an apartment in the building and was living there. I had tenants with long-term leases in some of the offices, my own staff in others, and a large commercial mortgage to pay each month. So my business, home, and all of my finances were tied up in this property. I was waking up at night in a sweat.

I told a close friend that I'd been trying to come up with some way to hold onto at least part of my original dream. But, truthfully, thinking about it further frustrated me, as it seemed like childish folly. There was no way I could have what I wanted. I wanted to stay in the building, keeping a few choice offices and my apartment, for as long as I wanted, and have absolutely NO financial responsibility for the building. Impossible!

My friend asked, "Have you meditated about it?" I had not. Back then I was new to meditating and visualizing, and I certainly didn't trust that if I asked for guidance, the answers would come.

But they did. Boy, did they ever!

My friend encouraged me to experiment. What did I have to lose? So, for about three weeks, first thing in the morning, I suspended reality. I visualized exactly what I wanted. I saw myself in the building, in my apartment and in my favorite offices, happy, carefree. I saw myself coaching and running groups, feeling professionally fulfilled, even elated.

I heard the phone ringing off the hook with interest in our coaching and therapy services. I saw lots of checks and credit card payments coming in and I saw myself easily, gratefully writing just one small outgoing check every month. I had free time and I was laughing more than I had in a long time. At the end of each meditation, I asked for a way to make this all come true—and I trusted it would.

One amazing morning the idea arrived. It covered the whole picture! I could sell the building to someone who wanted to continue to rent out individual offices. As part of the contract, I could set my own rents for my four favorite offices and for my apartment, and maintain them for as long as I wanted. I could stay on as the onsite building manager so I could be sure the building was kept up to my standards. Remarkably, this was the answer to everything I had almost dismissed as folly.

Next, I visualized the price I wanted for the building. I made some calls, putting the word out that the building was for sale at that price. Five weeks later, the building was sold, the contracts were signed for the exact amount I had visualized, less just $500. I got my own office rent-free, in exchange for managing the building. For the next four years I wrote one small monthly check for everything. I never paid another utility bill!

When I bought a house and moved from the apartment, the new owner of the building even paid me to be the "on-call" manager. With not much to do, it was like found money for another three years.

This experience made me a believer. Today, my friends call me the "Queen of Manifestation." It's a title I wear with great appreciation and faith in the power I now know I have to co-create the life I want. When I ask for what I want, the answers come. What a gift!

Defining What You Want

Empowerment means being able to create the life you want. But how do you define what it is that you want to create for yourself? Like a lot of people, you may have no idea what you want. If that is the case, it may be helpful to use a tool known as The Passion Test. Developed by Janet Attwood and Chris Attwood, this method leads you through a series of steps to first identify the things you love and care about most, then to distill from that list the five things that are most important to you—your passions.

Once you are clear about your passions, you can use them to guide you in creating a life that truly reflects your authentic values and goals. For example, you may begin the process by generating a list of ten things you would like to have in your life. By following the steps of The Passion Test, you refine and re-refine that list until you end with five core passions. You state them in the present tense, as if you are already living them out. Your list may look something like this:

1. I have a loving and satisfying relationship with my partner.
2. I live in a peaceful and nurturing home.
3. I am connected to Divine Source and to my own Divinity.
4. I fully express my creativity through art, dance, and music.
5. I work as a healer and help many people.

You then place copies of the list in several places where you are likely to see them —the bathroom mirror, refrigerator door, computer monitor—so that you are reminded of it several times each day. Your list serves as a guide, reminding you of what is most central to your life so that you make decisions that support your passions. This process is simple, and anyone can do it. Living in alignment with your true values can dramatically change your life.

The Power of the Present Moment

When you focus your attention upon the present moment, you give yourself the gift of *choice*. You observe what is happening right now, and your reactions to it. And right there, you get to decide what to do next. The instant you make that decision, you move from victimhood to empowerment.

Being in the present moment seems as if it would be simple, but it can actually be difficult for us to do. We live such fast-paced lives, filled with unrelenting stimulation, that it can be hard to sit still and be quiet. And we are so accustomed to thinking about the past or the future that it feels foreign to us to focus on the present moment. Our minds are like restless little monkeys, jumping and swinging here and there, constantly moving and hard to restrain. But when we are still, even for a few minutes, we create the space for our authentic selves, our true Divinity, to emerge.

You are a powerful being whose energy reaches far beyond you and into the world. The automatic thought processes of dwelling on the past or planning for the future prevent you from being present to your thoughts and feelings. And it's only by being in the present that you can consciously direct your thoughts toward what you want to create in your life.

In the next few chapters, we present the *Prescriptions*. These are specific suggestions to help you gain deeper understanding of your life, to help you clear the negative energy that can keep you feeling "stuck," and to empower you to manifest a life—and a *world*—full of love, joy, peace, and compassion.

Part Two

The Spiritual Prescriptions

5

Prescription #1:
Use Energy-Based Healing

Our first Spiritual Prescription is to use energy healing techniques. These techniques utilize Divine Energy, known as *chi* or *Q'i,* to help you heal physically, emotionally, and spiritually. *Chi* means "universal life force" and is understood to be that which gives us "the breath of life."

Energy healing techniques are gentle, non-invasive treatments that are relaxing and helpful to the immune system. By using them regularly, you will ease your way through these turbulent times. Our favorites are Reiki, BodyTalk, and Healing Touch, described in this chapter.

Reiki

As we discussed in Chapter 1, one of the most well-known forms of energy healing is Reiki. Reiki practitioners serve as conduits or channels for *chi* to be delivered to you through the practitioner's hands. The practitioner places his or her hands over your chakras, or energy centers, and this process opens each chakra and balances the flow of energy through your chakras. *Chi* naturally goes to the places in your body that are in need of healing and restores your system to health.

Leslie is not only a Reiki Master practitioner, but she receives Reiki treatments regularly from Melissa Hoffman, a very gifted healer and massage therapist in Cincinnati. Here, Leslie describes a Reiki session that was especially significant to her:

> When I lay down on the massage table, I took a few breaths and looked around the room. All the shades were drawn; the

room was dark save for the candle on the table to my left. A new age CD was playing softly in the background. I felt my body sink into the heated table pad. The heat soaked into my muscles, gently coaxing them into relaxed submission. I closed my eyes and took slow, deep breaths.

Melissa came into the room and began to scan my energy. She moved her hands over each chakra, starting above my head and moving down to my feet. Then she brought her hands back to my heart chakra, where she paused for a few moments. She reached into her pocket and pulled out a large crystal that hung from a long chain. She held the crystal above my heart chakra and let it dangle there to see how it reacted. If my heart chakra had been open, the crystal would have started moving in a circular direction. It didn't move. The chakra was apparently closed.

This surprised me. I hadn't noticed it being closed. Had I been numbing my feelings? The fact that I couldn't answer that question told me I had.

Melissa put the crystal back into her pocket and sat down on her stool. She slid both hands under my back, directly behind my heart chakra. Her hands felt warm underneath my back, as she gently pressed her fingertips into my skin. She slid her right hand out and placed it directly on top of my chest, over my heart chakra. She remained there, still, and then slowly began to move her hands in a slow, back and forth motion that gently rocked my upper body.

As she did this, I felt my heart begin to pound. It kept pounding for several seconds, and then gradually gave way to a surging sense of movement in my chest. It felt like a little river of energy that began to flow through my heart and down through the rest of my chakras.

I noticed a lump in my throat that caused me to inhale sharply. Tears sprang to my eyes and I began to cry, stifling the urge to sob. I couldn't hold it back and I started to sob. Between sobs, I told Melissa that my dog had died the previous week, unexpectedly and suddenly. I felt the pain of that loss pressing down on my chest, forcing me to cry until I could cry no more.

My heart ached physically until the crying burned itself out. Then I felt a deep stillness within me, a sense of utter peace, and the physical and emotional exhaustion that only comes with the release of intense pain. I took a deep breath, and it felt as if my cells were being cleansed and restored to life. Energy was flowing through me again, and I felt incredible relief.

No wonder my heart chakra had been closed! I had been unconsciously protecting myself from the pain of loss and grief. Once I allowed my heart chakra to open, though, the pain was able to move through my body and my healing could begin.

BodyTalk

BodyTalk is a body-based healing technique that involves re-establishing the natural connections between the various systems within the body. According to the International BodyTalk Association, exposure to daily stress disrupts these connections and causes your emotional and physical health to decline. By restoring the connections, BodyTalk helps your body and your emotions to naturally heal.

At the holistic healing center that was co-founded by Cathy and her colleague, Dr. Tammy Huber, BodyTalk treatment was going to be offered by energy healer Anne Steffen. In order to explore it as a possible resource for her clients, Cathy first had a BodyTalk session with Anne.

Cathy had been feeling depleted, and her stress level was fairly high. But the BodyTalk session restored her energy and she no longer felt stressed. Cathy referred several clients for BodyTalk sessions to augment their psychotherapy, and they found it facilitated their therapy.

At a recent conference for new authors, Cathy met Susie Steadman, the Australian author of the upcoming book, *Loud, Proud, and Unstoppable—A Rebel's Guide to Your Dream Career.* Susie had sought treatment with BodyTalk in order to overcome a somewhat debilitating fear. She offered to share her experiences with BodyTalk to illustrate how powerful the technique can be:

Susie had a terrible and unrealistic fear of riding as a passenger in cars. Her fear created a major problem for her, because she worked with well-known rock bands and toured with them all over the world. Since some of that time involved riding in cars, she experienced terror quite often.

She shared a semi-humorous example with us, in which she was being driven at 220 kph on the Autobahn in Germany. She was so scared that she drank an entire bottle of Rescue Remedy, a homeopathic remedy for anxiety that is usually taken in doses of one to two drops. She actually passed out after her "overdose," which led her eventually to seek other methods of overcoming her fear.

Susie's fear was also crippling other aspects of her life. She could not accept invitations to travel in someone else's vehicle, and was even terrified on public transport buses. And her fear was increasing as she grew older.

Someone recommended BodyTalk to her, and she decided to try it, despite feeling that it was "a little kooky." During the session, she lay on a massage table while someone used muscle testing to ask her body what issues it wanted or needed to be treated and where they were located in the body. After one session she was completely free of her car-riding fear.

Susie explained that she had been in two separate auto accidents as a child. One of them had been so traumatic for her that she did not speak for two months following the accident. Her present fear made sense in light of these auto accidents, but it was now inhibiting rather than protecting her. During her BodyTalk session, Susie felt her anxiety rise and she re-experienced the vulnerability she had felt as a child at the time of the accident.

But she did not feel overwhelmed by her feelings, and said the session was peaceful. She never had to talk about the experience. At the end of her session she felt "light, really different, like a weight was off her shoulders." Almost immediately she was able to ride as a passenger in a car without this unrealistic fear. It has never returned, but her senses are still in tune with any real or apparent danger.

Susie continues to get BodyTalk sessions to help her with the negative energies that she picks up while touring. She often returns from touring "feeling heavy and wanting to cry." After one thirty-minute session she is able to feel "totally alive again, like putting gas in the tank, filling (her) right up."

She also uses BodyTalk treatments to help manage her thyroid levels. She had thyroid cancer early in life and does not have a thyroid gland, so relies on thyroid replacement hormone. With BodyTalk, the facilitator can monitor the interaction of all the hormone glands, which assists with keeping her thyroid levels more "finely tuned" than they would be with blood tests alone.

Susie also shared that she recommended BodyTalk to a friend whose eight-year-old son had been diagnosed with cancer. This friend had lost a cousin to cancer when she was a child, and now she could not help believing that her son, too, would die. Her fear of this was affecting her ability to be with her son through his treatments.

Although she was a firm "nonbeliever" in such techniques, Susie's friend tried BodyTalk. Several sessions were needed, but they worked. She was soon able to deal with her son's cancer and his treatments, and he is now fully recovered.

Healing Touch

Healing Touch is an energy technique originally developed by Janet Mentgen, RN, BSN, a holistically centered nurse who studied and practiced various energy therapies for many years. Healing Touch practitioners use gentle touch to rebalance your energy field and restore your natural ability to heal (from http://www.healingtouchinternational.org).

During a healing touch session, the practitioner places their hands on or slightly above your body while you lie, fully clothed, on a massage table. The practitioner then moves their hands across and around your body to affect the energy within and surrounding you. This process rebalances your energy and allows it to flow normally. You feel deeply relaxed during the treatment, and may actually be able to feel the energy move and shift within and around you. Practitioners of Healing Touch recommend that you have regular sessions, because the effect is cumulative over time.

Healing Touch differs from Reiki in that it does not require an "attunement," the process by which Reiki practitioners receive the Reiki power symbols from the master teacher. These master symbols have been handed down from the ancient teachings of Reiki, and are said to empower the Reiki practitioners to receive and transmit the healing *chi* to others. Healing Touch does, however, follow a specific training process, which is taught in certification courses across the country.

Of all the energy healing methods, Healing Touch is the most widely accepted and practiced. It is used in hospitals and medical facilities throughout the world, and scientific studies have shown it to be quite effective. Medical doctors, psychotherapists, massage therapists, and other healers often recommend Healing Touch, either alone or in combination with more traditional treatment.

Healing Touch International can provide you with further information and training options, and can help you find a practitioner in your area.

Your body, your emotions, and your spirit are all impacted by the great energetic shift that is occurring in our world. The energy healing techniques we have presented in this chapter are effective, and using them regularly can provide gentle support to you as you experience the intense changes that are impacting all of us in this time of Universal transformation.

6

Prescription #2: Meditate!

Our second spiritual prescription is meditation. The term *meditation* is used to describe several different practices. It is often thought of as a spiritual or religious practice. We tend to associate Eastern spiritual traditions, especially Buddhism, with meditation, but it is also a part of many Western religions—including Christianity. Thomas Merton and other Christian "mystics," for example, engaged in deep contemplative practices—"silent, wordless prayer"—that expanded their awareness of the Divine within them (*Thomas Merton: Essential Writings,* p. 35).

In a spiritual or religious context, meditation serves to quiet the mind and deepen awareness of Spirit, God, or one's True Nature. However, the actual practice of meditation does not require any particular spiritual belief at all—in fact, atheists and "non-believers" can and do practice meditation. The benefits of meditation have been demonstrated in medicine and psychotherapy: it reduces stress hormone levels, boosts immunity, helps to reduce symptoms of anxiety, depression, and chronic pain.

It also improves memory, which could have favorable implications for age-related memory impairment and diseases, such as Alzheimer's, that cause memory loss. According to neuroscientist Daniel Siegel, MD, meditation regulates and stabilizes the mind. In the book *Mindsight*, he states that meditation can actually change the structure of your brain and promote the growth of new brain cells.

Aside from its medical and psychotherapeutic applications, meditation quiets the mind and develops a sense of inner peace and stability. It fosters a sense of oneness with Divinity and with all that is, and, simply put, makes life easier. In this chapter we'll explore several types of meditation from various cultural and spiritual traditions. We'll look first at *mindfulness,* an important component of meditation.

Mindfulness

An essential component of most forms of meditation is *mindfulness,* which can be understood simply as "awareness of present experience with acceptance," according to psychiatrist Ronald Siegel. This means that you become aware of your bodily sensations, thoughts, and feelings in the present moment, and that you accept them rather than fighting, avoiding, or judging them. You notice that you are thinking, that you are experiencing emotion, that you feel pain in your neck, or that you have an itch. You don't need to change anything at all; you are simply observing what is going on with you.

Thoughts and feelings can be like runaway trains. You start thinking about something, or you feel angry or sad, and before you know it, you are being carried away by your thoughts and emotions. You're on the train, speeding through the countryside, and you don't notice the view or even the fact that you're moving until you find yourself three hours later in another town, wondering where you are and how you got there.

If you start to pay attention to your experience in the present moment, you notice the thoughts that pop up in your mind, but you don't jump on the train and let them carry you away. You bring a sense of curiosity to your moment-by-moment experience, as though you are noticing things for the first time. You say to yourself, "Oh, I am thinking" and then you just watch your thoughts come and go like clouds passing through the sky. When you notice that you are feeling emotion, you say, "Oh, there is a feeling," and you watch what happens with the emotion as you observe it—but you don't jump on the train with it and let it whisk you off.

Likewise, if you notice discomfort or pain in your body, you say, "Oh, there is pain in (part of body)," and then you watch the pain. You watch it with light attention and curiosity, without letting it become all there is.

You can practice mindfulness by doing this simple exercise:

- Close your eyes and focus on your breathing, noticing how your chest and abdomen rise and fall with each breath.
- Do this for a few moments, and then turn your attention to your physical sensations in this moment. Notice the sensations of your body where it contacts the chair or couch. If you are able, feel your feet touching the floor or ground beneath you. See if you can feel your clothing against your skin.
- Become aware of any areas of your body in which you are experiencing discomfort. What is the quality of the discomfort: is it throbbing? Itching? Sharp or aching?
- Next, pay attention to what happens with the discomfort. Does it grow stronger? Does it grow weaker? Does it stay the same?

Most people find that the sensation changes in some way while they are observing it. Rather than remaining constant, it increases and diminishes. Interestingly, pain often eases when you simply observe it.

The same is true of your thoughts and feelings. If you become aware of them and you observe them in the present moment, you find that they also change. They come and go, rise and fall, like waves in an ocean. This awareness alone can help you to cope with pain, emotions, and thought patterns that seem overwhelming. If you study them, you discover that they are not the constant, unrelenting states you thought they were. Thoughts, feelings, and physical sensations are always changing, as is everything else in the Universe.

Mindfulness Based Stress Reduction

Mindfulness Based Stress Reduction (MBSR), pioneered by Jon Kabat-Zinn, PhD (*Full Catastrophe Living*, Bantam Dell, 1990), is a medically accepted strategy for managing pain, chronic illness, stress, and other physical and psychological issues. It consists of an eight-week training course that includes mindfulness instruction, group interaction, mindful yoga instruction and practice, and home practice CDs.

MBSR has been the subject of a great deal of clinical research, and has been found highly effective for helping people to manage a variety of conditions and challenges. MBSR programs exist throughout the country, and you can find more information and locate programs through the University of Massachusetts Center for Mindfulness in Medicine, Health Care, and Society, http://www.umassmed.edu.

In addition to founding Mindfulness Based Stress Reduction, Jon Kabat-Zinn's books and audio materials are excellent resources for mindfulness instruction that is practical and easy to follow. We have included some of these in the recommended resources list at the end of this book.

Types of Meditation

There are several "schools" of meditation, each with different origins and specific practices. We like to keep things relatively simple, and so will focus in this section on two well-known forms of meditation: *Shamatha*, or sitting meditation, and *Vipassana*, or insight meditation.

The Zen Buddhist practice of *Zazen,* or *Zen,* meditation is another well-known tradition, although we will not discuss it here. If you are interested in learning more about Zazen, we recommend the book *Zen Mind, Beginners Mind: Informal Talks on Zen Meditation and Practice* by Shunryu Suzuki.

Later in the chapter, we will also discuss walking meditation, "lovingkindness" meditation, and Transcendental Meditation.

Shamatha and Vipassana Meditation

Shamatha and Vipassana meditations are like cousins—related to one another but with some differences in genetic make-up. *Shamatha*, known as "peaceful abiding," is the process of sitting quietly with eyes open, focusing on your breathing, noticing when your mind wanders off, and bringing it back to your breathing. You use your breathing as your anchor or, to use a sports metaphor, your home plate. Then, when your mind takes off running around the bases—which are your thoughts and feelings—you stand there at home plate and watch. You note what your mind is doing, saying to yourself "thinking" or "feeling," and then you just gently coax it back to home plate, to your breathing.

What does it mean to "watch your breathing?" Well, it means to pay attention to the breath going into and out of your body, at a place where you notice it or feel it. For some people, it's the tip of their nose or their nostrils. You can feel the sensation of air going in and coming out there, a sort of coolness. Others prefer to watch the abdomen and/or chest rise and fall with each breath, as we referred to in our earlier mindfulness exercise. The point of it is to give you a central focus, so that your mind begins to settle down each time you bring it back to your breath after it has run off chasing thoughts and feelings.

Meditation teachers sometimes refer to our minds as "monkey minds," because they are like restless little monkeys jumping from one thing to another all the time. You can really see this when you do Shamatha meditation. The very first thing you notice is how much of the time you spend thinking. It is amazing to discover how many thoughts you have in a short amount of time! But you can train your mind to be still by bringing it back to your breathing, over and over again.

Minds are designed to think. Thoughts lead to feelings. Thoughts and feelings show up in your body. But your mind is supposed to be a tool, not the controller of your life. If you were to follow your thoughts for a while, you would see that most of them center upon something that has already happened—the past—or something that hasn't happened and may never happen—the future. Both the past and the future are *concepts*—ideas and thoughts that exist only in your mind. You can't point to "the past" or to "the future" because they are not there. Yet somehow those two concepts dominate most of your mind, most of the time.

Your breathing is the anchor that brings you back to the present moment. That is what is real. That is where your life is. When you inhabit the present moment, you create space within yourself for acceptance, compassion, and calm. And then you can decide what you want to do with your thoughts—your thought energy. Use it as your tool to create the present that you want, and to set the stage as best you can for the future that you would like to have.

Shamatha and Vipassana are both from the Buddhist tradition. Both schools of meditation view human suffering as caused by our resistance to what is. We think we will be happy when we get the job, graduate, have more money, get thinner, buy the next new electronic gadget, drive the new car … in the future. We carry anger over things that happened long ago, hauling around those memories and fueling them every day with the energy of our outrage and resentment … over the past. We long for things to be different, and believe that we are destined to be unhappy unless or until they are. And that is suffering.

The remedy to all of this is to be present right now. Meditation eases your suffering by teaching you to live in the moment.

Vipassana meditation builds upon Shamatha, by adding inquiry and observation—insight—to mindful awareness. When you calm your mind, you can begin to explore your habits of mind; you can come to understand that your thoughts often revolve around planning, remembering, or worrying. You realize that everything changes—your body, your thoughts, your feelings—and how you relate to those changes.

In *Seeking the Heart of Wisdom: The Path of Insight Meditation,* well-known meditation teachers Joseph Goldstein and Jack Kornfield say that meditation helps you to discover how you relate to your feelings. You learn how your feelings arise and how they affect your life. You start to see the stories you tell yourself, the assumptions you make based upon the events that occur in your life. For example, "He ignored me; it means he doesn't like me." "My house is a little messy, so my neighbors will think I'm a slob." These stories are constructed by you, in your own mind. When you meditate, you learn that you can drop the stories and turn your attention to what is true in this moment.

Shamatha and Vipassana meditation both help you to be less reactive to what happens around you. Meditation creates a sense of stability that you begin to carry with you into your daily life. When you are less reactive, you feel less tension and stress.

Walking Meditation

One frequent concern about learning to meditate is that it is too difficult to sit still and focus for any length of time. If you struggle with sitting meditation, you can try walking meditation. Beloved teacher Thich Nhat Hanh offers lovely instruction for walking meditation in his book *Peace Is Every Step.* You can try walking meditation yourself by doing one of the following simple practices.

For the first type of walking meditation, begin to walk at a comfortable pace and bring your attention to the details of your surroundings. Notice the leaves on the trees, their texture and shape, and how they feel to the touch. Look at the blades of grass, their color, how they vary in length, how they blow and bend with the breeze. Inhale the smells around you. Feel the temperature of the air. Stop to touch the bark on a tree, and feel its smoothness or roughness beneath your fingers. Notice the rhythm of your own breathing, the sound and feel of your footsteps as you walk. When your attention wanders, simply bring it back to your breathing and to your surroundings.

This easy exercise keeps you in the present moment by directing your attention to your senses. It can be invigorating and relaxing at the same time.

The second walking meditation is to focus upon the sensations of the actual movement of walking. As you walk, notice the sensation of lifting your leg, moving your foot forward, placing your foot on the ground, rolling it from heel to toe. This involves slowing down the motion considerably. If you like, you can simplify the exercise by noting the actions of lifting and placing each foot—with each step, attend to the feeling of lifting each foot and placing it on the ground, saying to yourself "lifting, placing" as you do it. It is helpful to do this practice in a limited space of about twenty feet, such as a hallway or short sidewalk, so that you walk to the end of it, turn around, and walk the other direction a few times. This keeps you focused on the sensations rather than on your surroundings.

Both forms of walking meditation serve to calm your mind while moving your body, and both are effective practices on their own or along with other forms of meditation. On the spiritual level, meditation fosters awareness of the connection between all humans, all beings, and the earth. It cultivates compassion toward yourself and toward others. As meditation teacher and author Sharon Salzberg says, "Resting fully in the present is the source of this happiness. We open to our own experience, and inevitably that opens us to others" (*Lovingkindness*, p. 17).

Lovingkindness Meditation

Metta, or "lovingkindness," describes an open, unconditional love and kindness that embraces all that is. It is boundless compassion that is not based upon conditions—that is, upon someone doing something or being something in relation to us. Likewise, it means having that same unconditional love and kindness for ourselves, as we are.

The Buddha taught metta meditation as an antidote to fear. According to Buddhist legend, Buddha sent a group of monks into a forest to meditate. The forest was filled with "tree spirits," who tried to scare the monks away by appearing to them as monsters and ghouls that shrieked and smelled horrible. When the monks ran back to the Buddha in terror, he sent them back into the forest, saying that he would provide them with the only protection they would need.

He then taught them the Metta Prayer, which he instructed them to recite and to practice. The monks did as they were told, re-entering the forest and practicing metta. The tree spirits were so moved by the loving energy that filled the forest that they stopped scaring the monks and decided to care for them and provide for their needs (*Lovingkindness,* p. 20).

To do Lovingkindness Meditation, you must begin with yourself. As Sharon Salzberg says, "Spirituality based on self-hatred can never sustain itself" (p. 26). For this reason, you offer lovingkindness to yourself before you extend it to others.

In a workshop with Sharon Salzberg in Colorado, Leslie learned the following version of metta meditation:

Begin by closing your eyes, and imagine yourself in the middle of a circle. Surrounding you are all the people and animals and spirits and deceased loved ones who have ever loved you. You are sitting there as all of them gaze upon you with great love, and they are saying to you:

May you be safe,
May you be happy,
May you be healthy,
May you be peaceful.

They repeat this prayer to you several times, and you begin to say it for yourself:

May I be safe,
May I be happy,
May I be healthy,
May I be peaceful.

Next, call to mind someone for whom you feel respect and deep gratitude. Recite the same prayer to them:

May you be safe,
May you be happy,
May you be healthy,
May you be peaceful.

Repeat the prayer several times for this person. Then, call to mind someone who is a beloved friend. Recite the prayer to them:

May you be safe … .

When you have gently extended this prayer to them, think of someone who is neutral to you, such as the mail carrier or the cashier at the grocery. Repeat the prayer to them a few times, noticing how your heart begins to open toward them.

Next, choose someone with whom you have been in conflict, or toward whom you have felt anger or fear. Try not to choose someone who has hurt you severely at first. Think of the things that are good about this person. Extend the prayer to them, repeating it several times:

May you be safe,
May you be happy,
May you be healthy,
May you be peaceful.

Notice as you do this how the constriction around your heart begins to relax and soften. This may take a while, so be patient with yourself. It may even take a few days and a few meditation sessions to be able to feel this gradual opening. Note how you feel when it finally happens.

Note: *You can also do this exercise by sending metta to a part of yourself that you have difficulty with, such as anger, jealousy, or some aspect of your body.*

Finally, extend the metta prayer to all beings everywhere. You can break them up into categories, such as:

May all humans be safe . . .
May all animals be safe . . .
May all creatures be safe . . .

And last,

May all beings everywhere, without exception, be safe...

You can use other words and phrases in place of these if you like. Cathy uses a Lovingkindness Prayer she learned from Joan Borysenko when she spoke in Cincinnati:

May I be at peace,
May I know the beauty of my own true nature,

May my heart remain open,
May I be healed.
May you be at peace, (you may insert a particular name here).
May you know the beauty of your own true nature.
May your heart remain open.
May you be healed.
May everyone on earth be at peace.
May everyone know the beauty of their own true nature.
May everyone's hearts remain open.
May everyone be healed.

Masaru Emoto's water crystal photographs illustrate the beauty and power of the positive energy that is generated by prayers such as the Metta Prayer. These photos show water before and then after a Buddhist prayer was spoken over the water.

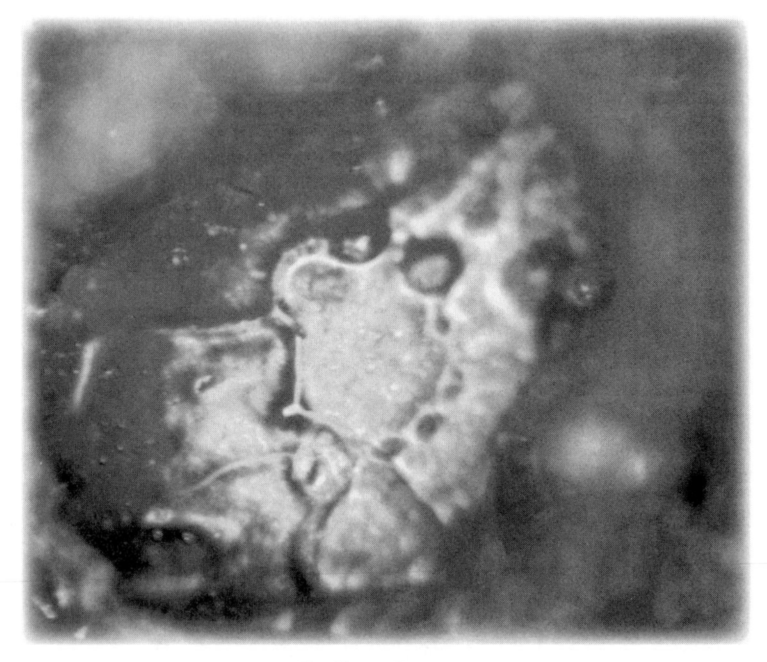

Before Prayer

After Prayer

The Lovingkindness Meditation is such a beautiful, heart-opening, and deeply compassionate practice! When you extend it toward yourself, lovingkindness softens the hard edges of self-criticism and allows self-acceptance to emerge. If you are in conflict with someone else, lovingkindness can bridge the divisions caused by anger, jealousy, resentment, and hurt. This gentle practice will lead you to the unconditional compassion and acceptance that is your True Nature.

Transcendental Meditation

Transcendental Meditation (TM) is a world-renowned method of meditation that comes from the Vedic tradition of enlightenment in India. It was brought to the Western world by Maharishi Mahesh Yogi about fifty years ago, and has been the subject of extensive research into its effects and benefits. Like other forms of meditation, it has been shown to reduce anxiety and stress, and to have other benefits for the brain and the body. It enjoyed a surge in popularity in the 1970s, and is still practiced by millions of people around the world.

TM requires specific training that is offered through courses taught by certified TM teachers. TM practitioners describe it as an "effortless practice," in which the mind is taught to transcend the constant stream of thoughts that we typically experience. Going beyond the thinking mind allows someone to enter a state of natural bliss and inner peace (http://www. tm.org).

Oprah Winfrey visited and did a televised feature about Fairfield, Iowa, a city where 20 percent of the population practices Transcendental Meditation—about 3000 people. The meditator community is strong, dedicated to the development of human potential. Centered around Maharishi University of Management, they have established a "consciousness-based" educational system that goes from pre-school to PhD level. TM is taught at every level, beginning with kindergarten; children under the age of ten start with a "walking meditation" that uses a "word of wisdom," and progress to a sitting mantra meditation with eyes closed as they get older. Advanced meditators stop twice each day to gather and meditate in the university's two huge meditation domes.

Janet Bray Attwood, one of the founders of The Passion Test, lives in Fairfield and says that you can feel the energy change as you drive near the town, since the whole community vibrates at a high frequency. Cathy asked Janet for an interview when we were writing this book, and she graciously agreed.

Janet is the co-author of the *New York Times* bestseller *The Passion Test: The Effortless Path to Discovering Your Life Purpose.* She speaks, teaches, and conducts workshops around the world, and is the recipient of The President's Volunteer Service Award, the highest presidential award for service. To say that she is a powerhouse is an understatement. Below, Cathy shares Janet's story with us:

> Forty years ago, Janet was strung out on drugs. She used LSD to get high, led a "pretty crazy" life, and was miserable. Her brother, whom she called in tears one day, arrived in San Jose, California to rescue her. He drove her to Santa Barbara, California, they found a house to rent together, and he introduced her to Transcendental Meditation.

Transcendental Meditation (TM) was a popular system of meditation at that time, and her brother practiced it regularly. He believed it could help Janet, and suggested that she receive the training. It was, quite literally, the answer to her prayers. Janet credits TM with transforming her life.

The first time she tried it, Janet recognized that what she had sought by using drugs was exactly what TM provided. Since that day, she has been practicing TM twice a day.

TM is a particular way of meditating that allows a person to transcend, or go beyond the mind's "thinking process." This experience, Janet says, is very restful. A great deal of research—more than 600 scientific studies—has been conducted on TM by top colleges and universities around the world, and its benefits have been well documented. Researchers have found that by doing TM twice a day, a person can clear their mind and body of stress that has accumulated over a lifetime.

Janet refers to TM as "the effortless practice." Although she loves and practices the Transcendental Meditation technique, she states that "any meditation that transcends or goes beyond the thinking process could be called 'transcendental.'"

Janet is committed to her meditation practice, and it has become central to her life. She has been fortunate to travel to different parts of the globe and study directly with Maharishi Mahesh Yogi, the founder of Transcendental Meditation. She considers him to be her spiritual teacher. She later spent several years traveling throughout India interviewing significant gurus and teachers, which was something she had always dreamed of doing. She wanted to learn what they were most passionate about. It was no surprise to Janet when she found that for most yogis, their passion was simply "to know thyself."

Today she lives in Fairfield, Iowa, and is a "Governor of the Age of Enlightenment" (one who is both a teacher of TM and who practices Maharishi's advanced TM and TM-Sidhi program).

Janet says that teenagers in Fairfield are open hearted, and their faces do not bear signs of stress. Their strong foundation of meditation leads to their extraordinary spiritual growth; Janet says that it is "humbling" to be with a sixteen-year-old from Fairfield because their inner wisdom is so great.

I interviewed Janet because she has been a significant influence in my life, and the lives of so many others. She lives her meditation, experiencing the world with a full and open heart, seeing the good in everyone she meets. It is the creative force behind all that she does. In Janet's words, "the world is as you are." Those who meet Janet find her to be one of the most loving people they have ever encountered.

I asked Janet what, in her eyes, were the benefits of regular meditation practice. She described these as clarity of vision, reduction of stress, a full heart, inner wisdom, and an awareness that you are "part and parcel of the unified field. Once you transcend the thinking process, you experience this 'unbounded awareness,' and you are able to bring that unbounded awareness into your daily life," she said.

Janet used the metaphor of a white cloth being dipped in red dye each day and then left in the sun to bleach. Day after day the cloth is dipped in the red dye, then hung to dry, until eventually the cloth becomes colorfast. In that same way, when a person practices Transcendental Meditation on a regular basis, they experience the unboundedness of the Unified Field, the oneness of everything. They experience deep rest that releases deeply rooted stress, until eventually the inner and outer experience become one and the same.

Being Present

Being in the present moment is the key to all true transformation. Many readers may be familiar with Eckhart Tolle's works, *The Power of Now* and *A New Earth* (which we referred to in an earlier chapter). In *The Power of Now,* Tolle tells the story of feeling depressed and suicidal several years ago, when the sudden insight came to him that he was more than just his thoughts and feelings—that he was actually capable of observing his thoughts, feelings, and sensations in the present moment without being controlled by them.

His relief was so profound that he became blissfully content to simply be in and to accept the present moment—and it saved his life. It was the breakthrough that led him to become a spiritual teacher who has reached and touched the lives of millions of people. The present moment became the key to enlightenment.

Adyashanti, a gifted spiritual and meditation teacher, is a favorite of Cathy's. His meditation centers upon acceptance of all that is, allowing everything to be as it is. There is nothing to learn, no effort to be anything other than who you are in the moment. The simple permission to be as you are provides relief from the constant pressure of trying to be perfect or to do things "right."

According to transformational healer Panache Desai, the key to inner peace is to embrace who you are, exactly as you are (http://www.panachedesai.com). There is nothing about you that is broken, nothing that needs to be fixed. He encourages people to embrace all the things that they don't like about themselves—their illnesses, their feelings of inadequacy, the thoughts and feelings that they want to avoid. The act of embracing what they dislike about themselves actually raises their vibration, which often causes the things they didn't like to shift and change of their own accord.

Meditation is a way to open the door to self-acceptance and greater compassion for all that is. Below, we provide a list of meditation resources (see Bibliography for detail) that we have found helpful. Some of them exist in both print and audio format. By no means is this an exhaustive list; there are many forms of meditation, and the key is to find one that feels comfortable for you.

- *Seeking the Heart of Wisdom: The Path of Insight Meditation,* Joseph Goldstein and Jack Kornfield.
- *The Heart of the Buddha's Teachings: Transforming Suffering into Peace, Joy, and Liberation,* Thich Nhat Hanh.
- *Turning the Mind Into an Ally,* Sakyong Mipham.
- *Start Where You Are: A Guide to Compassionate Living,* Pema Chodron.

- *Lovingkindness: The Revolutionary Art of Happiness,* Sharon Salzberg.
- *Wherever You Go, There You Are: Mindfulness Meditation in Everyday Life,* Jon Kabat-Zinn.
- *Mindfulness for Beginners: Reclaiming the Present Moment—and Your Life,* Jon Kabat-Zinn.
- *Peace is Every Step: The Path of Mindfulness in Everyday Life,* Thich Nhat Hanh.
- *True Meditation,* Adyashanti, Sounds True Audio CD, Boulder, CO, 2006. (There is an audio CD with two meditations that comes with this book.)
- *Falling Into Grace: Insights on the End of Suffering,* Adyashanti. (This book comes in an audio version as well.)

7

Prescription #3: Develop Self-Compassion

Self-compassion, our third spiritual prescription, forms the critical foundation in the creation of positive energy within your life. You are Divinity itself; what is there in Divinity to criticize?

The dark energy of self-loathing is heavy and dense, toxic to your mind, your body, and your spirit. Earlier in the book, you learned through Masaru Emoto's photos of water crystals how negative words affected water—and you are made mostly of water! Intolerance and harshness toward yourself has the same impact on your energy and health that it would on water.

Most of us are naturally able to be compassionate toward children. For this reason we encourage people to begin learning self-compassion by first developing it toward their child selves—that is, toward the children they once were. It's easy to recognize that a child is vulnerable and impressionable, and that messages of hatred or rejection can deeply wound them. It's also easy to understand that children need to feel loved and to know that they are safe. By connecting with their inner child, many people are able to feel self-love, which is vital to their healing.

For some people, though, thinking of themselves as children can bring up feelings of intolerance or even self-loathing. They blame themselves for the actions of the adults who surrounded them as children, and condemn themselves for not having behaved or responded differently to circumstances.

If the idea of feeling compassion for your child self triggers feelings of disgust for you, or if you feel hatred or repulsion toward your child self, please be gentle with yourself. This merely suggests that from the earliest moment you can remember, you did not feel loved or worthy of love. People who have suffered early neglect or trauma sometimes experience this.

We encourage you to seek a therapist to help you to work through these feelings, because research has shown time and time again that the therapy relationship is a healing experience. When you feel a good connection with your therapist, you get the chance to feel safe, supported, and valued—all things that you likely did not experience as a child. We call it a corrective experience, because it corrects some of the negative beliefs and feelings you have about yourself.

When a client experienced anger or even hatred toward the child they once had been, Leslie would often encourage them to spend some time observing children around the same age that they (the client) would have been at the time they were abused or mistreated. The client was asked to pay particular attention to the children's small size, how they played, the things they talked about. Often the client would come back to therapy and exclaim, "They are so little!" or "They are so innocent!"

Once a client was able to understand that they were every bit as small and innocent when they were young, they could usually admit that their expectations of themselves as children had been unreasonable. This made it possible for them to consider that they deserved compassion instead of derision.

You can also begin to cultivate self-compassion by loving and nurturing an animal. Often we feel able to love and care for an animal, because animals love us openly and unconditionally. As you care for an animal, you can begin to notice yourself providing the sort of loving care with which you would like to have been treated as a child. This awareness can be the bridge that leads, eventually, to learning to nurture yourself with the same type of loving care.

There are additional ways to develop compassion for yourself. Cathy originally learned the following technique from a guided meditation by Rick Carson, author of *Taming Your Gremlin*. We have made some changes in the meditation, but its basis is still the same. Here is the instruction:

Begin by sitting comfortably in a location where you will not be disturbed. Allow your focus to rest on your breath. Notice your belly rise as you breathe in and fall as you breathe out. Allow your thoughts to naturally slow down, as you simply breathe and relax.

When you are breathing gently, and you feel relaxed and calm, allow an image to float into your mind. That image is you as a small child. You may be a tiny baby, a toddler, or any age up to five years old. Now see yourself as an adult, and allow your little child self to either sit in your lap or to face you and hold your hand.

Take your time and just look at the child, noticing his or her hair, face, eyes, and how big or small the child is. See if you can get a sense of what the child is feeling. If you are not sure, simply ask them. Focus on your heart, and imagine a beam of soft light that connects your heart with the child's heart. Let yourself rest in that soft connection for a moment.

As you are able, ask your child the question, "What do you most want or need from me right now?" Just listen quietly and see what arises. Your inner child may not yet feel close enough to you to talk with you. If so, that is fine. Understand that you may feel like a stranger to the child at this point. Simply let the child know that you are here to learn about him or her, and that you would like to be a good friend, or maybe a good parent, to them.

If you find that you feel emotional while you are connecting with this child, do not worry. This is perfectly normal. Just notice what you feel. Try not to judge any part of this experience.

If the child says she or he does need something specific from you, such as a hug, reassurance, or encouragement, please give it to them. You may need to say comforting words to the child. Notice what the child seems to be feeling. That is most likely the way you felt when you were actually that age.

When you feel ready to disconnect from your inner child, tell the child that you are going to be leaving soon but that you will be back anytime the child wants or needs you. And if it feels true to say so, tell the child you love them and that you will always be there for them. Do not force yourself to say this if it does not feel true to you. You may just simply not feel it yet, and that is okay. Perhaps you will at another time. Try at least to let the child know that you will be back sometime to check on them.

When you are ready, gently bring yourself back into the present by noticing the sounds in the room. Feel your body touching the chair or surface that you are sitting on. Notice the temperature of the air in the room. Then slowly open your eyes.

People often experience powerful feelings during this meditation. It opens the heart to emotions that may have been locked away for years. Bringing these feelings out of hiding is an important first step in learning to accept that they, like you, were an innocent and lovable child.

Shaina Noll, a therapist in New Mexico, has assembled a collection of songs entitled *Songs for the Inner Child*. Her music is gentle and soothing, and makes it easier for you to connect with your child self in a compassionate way. One of the songs, "You Can Relax Now," is reprinted here with permission of the writer and the publicist, words and music by Susan McCullen:

You can relax now
C'mon and open your eyes
Breathe deeply now
I am with you
Oh my sweet sweet child
Who do you think you are?
You are a child of God
And that will never change.
You had a dream, you misunderstood
You thought you were separate
But now you hear my voice and
You can relax now
C'mon and open your eyes
Breathe deeply now
I am with you
You are the love of my life
You are my one creation
You are eternity
And that will never change.

If we are to heal the world, we must first heal ourselves. Self-compassion is an indispensable part of that healing.

8

Prescription #4: Appreciate Your Body

"The body is a temple." How do you react when you read that sentence? Some of us rarely think about our bodies, except to criticize them. And no wonder—our culture teaches us that we must look a certain way in order to be loved. Such emphasis on appearance can lead us to forget that our bodies serve a sacred purpose: they are the earthly vehicles that house our souls in this physical world. This, then, is the fourth spiritual prescription: appreciate your body.

Part of your purpose here on earth is to enjoy the physical world. Your body enables you to experience the pleasures of the world through touch, taste, sight, smell, and sound. You are able to move your body, to express and to feel emotion in your body. It is a wondrous machine that carries out incredibly complicated functions in order to give you the gift of earthly life. When you pause to consider your body from this perspective, you come to understand that it is vital to care for and nurture it.

We recommend that any healing method that focuses on the emotions also include a component of treatment that focuses on the body. After all, body, mind, and spirit are one unified system. Your body holds cellular and muscular memory, and has absorbed all of your earthly experiences. Healing methods that focus on the body can help your body to release stress, trauma, toxins, and unhelpful muscular and skeletal patterns.

In this chapter, we'll talk about some of the most significant practices we've found to heal and care for the body, including massage, reflexology, CranioSacral Therapy, movement, grounding, yoga—and sleep!

Massage and Reflexology

Massage involves the manipulation of muscles through pressing, kneading, rolling, rubbing, and/or stretching. It promotes relaxation, provides pain relief, stimulates blood flow, and relieves stress. Massage therapy can be a helpful adjunct to psychotherapy and to other forms of healing. It is a gentle way to reconnect with your body, to nurture and heal your body, and help it to let go of pain and toxic energy. Before you choose a massage therapist, however, you should know what type of massage the therapist offers and what training and qualifications they have.

One of the most common forms of massage is Swedish, which uses long soft stroking, kneading, and tapping. It focuses on the outer layer of muscles, stimulates blood flow, and relieves muscle tension. If you have never had a massage, Swedish massage is a good place to start.

In contrast, Deep Tissue massage uses deeper, more focused pressure on muscles and tissues. It is ideal for treating chronic muscle tension or postural patterns that cause frequent or ongoing pain. As the massage therapist kneads and presses on your body's problem areas, muscle spasms and stiffness are released. It can be a bit painful when the therapist works on your tender spots, but the relief you feel afterward is significant.

Shiatsu massage involves using pressure on the body's acupressure points to release blocked energy and restore the body's flow of *chi*, life force energy. Some massage therapists use more intense pressure on the acupressure points than do others, so it's helpful to ask the therapist how much pressure they use prior to scheduling your massage.

Neuromuscular massage treats the underlying causes of chronic pain by applying pressure to your trigger points, which are tender points on the body that can be painful to the touch. Working with the trigger points helps to relieve nerve compression, postural issues, and pain caused by repetitive movement.

For clients who have experienced sexual trauma, massage therapy can be especially helpful. When someone has been sexually abused or assaulted, they often learn to dislike their body, or to blame it for the abuse. Massage therapy offers them a way to positively reconnect with their body. It can also be a chance for them to experience safe, nurturing touch.

If you have been abused and you are in psychotherapy, it's a good idea to discuss the option of massage therapy with your counselor or therapist before considering massage therapy. It is best to find a massage therapist who has experience in working with sexual trauma. And if you have never had a massage, we suggest that you try Swedish or another lighter method at first.

If massage therapy feels a little too intimidating, reflexology may be a good alternative. Reflexology uses hand, thumb, and finger pressure along with massage on specific areas of your feet. These areas correspond to all of the organs, tissues, and systems in your body. Reflexology is designed to relieve pain and to promote overall health. See http://www.webmd.com/balance/massage-therapy-styles-and-health-benefits.

Massage and reflexology offer multiple benefits for your emotional and physical health. Both help you to connect with and appreciate your body, to soothe stress, and to relieve pain. When you care for your body, you also nurture your spirit.

CranioSacral Therapy (CST)

CranioSacral Therapy (CST) was developed by osteopathic physician John E. Upledger, based upon years of clinical research and testing in biomechanics at the University of Michigan. It is a system of gentle touch used to release tension and relieve pain by correcting problems in the soft tissues and the fluid surrounding the brain and spinal cord. These tissues—the fascial membranes—and the cerebrospinal fluid make up the body's craniosacral system, and are connected to every structure in the body.

Everyday stresses on your body cause restrictions and disruptions in its craniosacral system, which affect the functioning of the nervous system and of your body as a whole. CST practitioners use their hands to lightly touch areas of your body in order to detect any disruptions in your craniosacral system. They also place one or both hands under your sacrum (thus the "sacral" in craniosacral). They then apply very gentle pressure to these areas, which releases tension and restriction in the tissues. Your craniosacral system is restored to normal functioning, and pain that has been held deep within your body is relieved (The Upledger Institute website, http://www.Upledger.com)

It's amazing that a system of light touch can have such a powerful effect, but it does. There is a noticeable release of tension—Leslie refers to it as a "full-body sigh." It relaxes the body and the mind, and promotes a sense of peace and well-being. CST is sometimes practiced in conjunction with energy work, massage therapy, or other holistic treatments. According to the Upledger Institute, CranioSacral Therapy helps boost immune functioning, and can help to alleviate chronic pain, sports injuries, and even neurological impairment.

Put Some Movement in It!

Exercise is among the very first recommendations we make for clients who suffer from stress, depression, low energy, anxiety, and a host of other issues. Leslie recalls the sage advice of one therapist who routinely suggested to her clients that they "put some movement in it" when they were feeling stuck, fearful, anxious, angry, or depressed. The notion of getting off the couch and getting your body moving may be the last thing you want to do, but it is often the best and fastest route to feeling better.

When you "put some movement in it," you literally move stuck energy through your body. Whether you walk, run, jump rope, cycle, swim, or do push-ups, you are doing *something*. And you are benefiting your body in a myriad of ways.

Exercise elevates levels of neurotransmitters, brain chemicals that are linked to mood and anxiety. By raising those levels, exercise improves your mood and reduces anxiety. It also improves your memory, helps to control cravings, and stimulates the "feel-good" chemicals in your brain known as endorphins. Perhaps most amazing is the fact that exercise is actually good for the brain. It helps the brain to form new connections, and scientists believe that it may actually stimulate the growth of new brain cells!

Aside from these benefits, exercise can be a source of empowerment. Physical strength and fitness provide an antidote to feelings of helplessness and powerlessness. As fitness improves, energy and self-confidence follow suit.

Martial arts and self-defense training can be particularly useful methods of increasing physical and mental strength for people—especially women—who have felt unable to defend themselves from abuse, assault, or other traumatic experiences. Some women find that through this type of training, they connect with inner courage that they did not know they had. In self-defense training, male trainers often play the role of the "attacker" so that a woman can practice self-defense techniques. Even the experience of saying a loud "NO!" to the trainer/"attacker" as she practices self-defense can be enormously empowering for a female trainee. We encourage our clients who seek self-defense training to talk with their trainers ahead of time so that yelling "NO!" is included in the training.

For one of Cathy's clients, just saying "No!" was an important turning point in her therapy. She started by simply saying no to her trainer if he wanted her to do more reps than she felt she could do. It energized her, and she no longer viewed herself as a victim. Instead, she felt empowered and gained more confidence in her inner strength.

Another way to liberate your energy and move your body is through dance. Even if you think you can't dance, you can move your body to express emotion, get your energy flowing, and change your perspective. Dancing spontaneously, completely without structure, allows your body to follow its natural pattern of movement and expression, which helps to release blocked energy and expands your sense of wholeness and connection with all that is.

Transformational leader Lisa Michaels wrote *Natural Rhythms* and created a program of the same name to teach people to pay attention to the rhythms of nature in order to increase their success in all areas of their lives. She uses dance as a way to facilitate learning, and says that for accelerated learning to occur or for major emotional shifts to be facilitated, one needs to "be open to dancing when the energy needs to move through you" (p. 24). According to Lisa, dance unifies the energies of spirit and the physical world, enabling you to use that energy to create your life as you want it to be.

The simple act of walking can also provide a shift in energy and perspective. In our automated society, we have lost the art of walking as a means of releasing frustration, blocked energy, and communion with nature. The confines of a room or a building tend to magnify the intensity of your problems, and make them seem overwhelming or impossible to address. When you go outside to walk, you see your problems under the big sky and discover that they are not as significant as they had appeared to be.

Walking while thinking about a problem or concern can be a sort of "simple EMDR" (see Chapter 13). It helps your brain to process experience, memory, and information, all of which enhances your ability to problem-solve. A brisk walking pace forces you to breathe, and breathing oxygenates the tissues and enables your brain to function. It also interrupts and soothes the alarm or trauma reaction and calms both body and mind.

Grounding

Your body is, quite literally, what grounds you to the earth. It connects your soul to the earth, and the earth's energy to your own. Remembering your energetic connection to the earth and centering yourself within it is the process that is referred to as *grounding*. It is helpful for bringing your awareness into the present moment, becoming aware of your body and its connection to the earth. If you are feeling anxious, fearful, or scattered, grounding can have an immediately soothing effect on your body and your emotions.

John Friedlander and Gloria Hemsher discuss grounding as a means of connecting to your personal power. In their book, *Psychic Psychology: Energy Skills for Life and Relationship,* they suggest a method of grounding, which we have adapted with their permission, in which you drop an imaginary grounding cord from your genitals down into the center of the earth. For women, they encourage "female grounding," in which you drop the cord from each ovary, the uterus, and your sciatic nerve into the base of your spine, and then into the center of the earth (adapted from Psychic Psychology, pp. 69-74).

Over time, we have learned that the most helpful way to stay emotionally balanced and centered is to ground yourself deeply into the earth and then release negative energy through your grounding cord.

A quick and simple way to ground yourself is to simply focus on the sensations of your feet on the ground. You can also squat down and touch the ground, or lie down on the ground. As you directly experience through your senses your connection to the earth, you feel supported and held securely in the safety and stability of the earth.

Our friend and yoga instructor Irena Miller learned the personal and professional importance of grounding to her overall health. She shares her story below:

> When I became a yoga instructor, I felt a strong desire to alleviate my students' suffering. I was able to sense their emotional, physical, and spiritual pain, and wanted so much to help them that I let them connect to me energetically. I took on their feelings and even picked up their physical injuries! If their lower back went out, mine did, too. If they were sad, I became sad as well. As a result, my heart center was exhausted after every class, to the point that it was physically painful. My chest ached.
>
> When I figured out what was going on—that I was allowing my students to "cord" their energy to mine and thus drain me energetically—I consulted with my energy healer Anne Steffen. She taught me how to ground myself energetically, and how to create healthy boundaries around my energy. I learned that when we are

> not grounded, we're more likely to absorb other people's energy and make it our own. This is not healthy for us or for them!
>
> Now when I teach, I am able to support and guide my students in a grounded, healthy way. After classes, all of us leave feeling empowered and energetic. Learning how to ground myself was a huge turning point for me. If I hadn't discovered why I felt so drained, I would have had to stop teaching—something I love to do!

Grounding is particularly important for those who have been abused or traumatized. The pain of those experiences often leads to what Leslie calls the "floating-head syndrome," in which awareness and attention are limited to thoughts and emotions, and everything below the neck is ignored. You can only be fully alive if you maintain connection with body, mind, and spirit. Learning to ground may require effort and practice, but it is centering and stabilizing. Remember to stop once in awhile, and notice that you have feet, legs, arms, and a torso, in addition to a head. You are body, mind, and spirit, all connected to one another and to this earth that sustains us.

Yoga

The ancient practice of yoga is a form of moving meditation that can relax and restore body and mind. It usually involves moving your body into and holding various poses, sometimes complex, that require your full attention. It is difficult to think about other things when you are focused on finding and holding a yoga pose. Yoga naturally encourages you to breathe deeply, which delivers oxygen to your muscles and tissues and encourages relaxation.

Yoga also helps your body by increasing strength and flexibility. It is particularly useful if the constant stream of thoughts in your mind makes it difficult for you to relax. It offers the benefits of physical exercise while quieting the mind.

Different types of yoga emphasize different aspects of the practice. *Ashtanga* yoga is a bit more exercise oriented, and uses poses that progress from least to most strenuous and require more intense physical effort. *Anusara* yoga, on the other hand, follows a slower pace and emphasizes alignment of the body, breathing, and opening the heart. It can be quite helpful to people who are working through emotionally painful issues.

Sleep

Sleep is an essential part of taking care of your body. Unfortunately, our culture doesn't seem to appreciate the value of sleep. Instead, we tend to see it as a good thing when people sleep less but do more. We view these people as "go-getters," ambitious and determined to excel. In reality, however, most people in our country are sleep deprived, and this has negative consequences for their physical and emotional health.

Sleep is essential because it gives your bodily systems time to recover from the stresses of daily life, and gives your brain the necessary time to process the day's activities and information. It allows your immune system to function optimally, and provides the rest necessary for muscle growth and recovery. It also counteracts the effects of mental stress on your body.

Have you ever noticed that when you are going through something very difficult or painful, you feel more fatigued? That's because you actually need extra sleep during such times. Our clients who are grieving a significant loss, such as the death of a partner or a pet, often ask us why they feel so physically and mentally exhausted. Grief and other difficult emotions take a toll on your body, too.

If you have a hard time sleeping when you are upset, you may find it helpful to use soft music, relaxing imagery, meditation, or safe herbal supplements that promote sleep. Chamomile tea is soothing just before bedtime, as is a warm bath. Valerian and melatonin are two commonly used herbal sleep aids that are available over the counter. It is always important, though, to talk with your physician before taking any herbal supplement.

You are particularly vulnerable to illness when you are emotionally upset or under stress, because your immune system is weakened by stress. During these turbulent times, it is wise to make sleep a priority—and to get extra sleep if you can.

Your brain processes information during REM (rapid eye movement) sleep. A single cycle of REM sleep must be preceded by sixty minutes of uninterrupted sleep—and you need to have more than one REM cycle each night! So if you wake up repeatedly during the night, you are likely not getting enough REM sleep.

In the book *You Staying Young*, Drs. Michael Roizen and Mehmet Oz state that, "When people don't sleep for three or more days on end, they become psychotic: that's why so many forms of torture involve sleep deprivation" (p. 187). Sleep deprivation also causes impaired concentration, and leaves people more vulnerable to other mental health issues, such as depression, anxiety, and substance abuse, according to Daniel Amen in *Healing Anxiety and Depression*.

The age-old advice to "sleep on it" when you are upset, stressed, or trying to make a difficult decision is good advice. Extra sleep makes everything a little bit easier to handle. Your ability to think clearly and make sound decisions is much improved if you get good, sound sleep. As an added bonus, there is evidence that getting enough sleep is helpful in maintaining healthy body weight. Stress releases chemicals that cause the body to gain weight, and adequate sleep can counter that effect, according to Drs. Roizen and Oz (*You Staying Young*, p. 190).

In order for you to get enough sleep, you have to make time for sleep. Go to bed at a time that allows you to sleep seven to nine hours each night. It's also helpful to avoid caffeine after mid-afternoon, and to make certain that the room in which you sleep is dark and cool. And while it is hard to do, it is wise to set a regular schedule for going to sleep and waking up.

Massage, reflexology, CranioSacral Therapy, grounding, movement, and yoga are excellent ways to replenish your body with healing, life-giving energy. And sleep is essential for your overall health. Take care of your body, for it is the temple that houses your soul.

9

Prescription #5: Clear Your Negative Energy

As we learned in Chapter 1, we create some of our own suffering by focusing on negative thoughts and feelings. According to Patricia Cota-Robles in her book *Who Am I? Why Am I Here?,* humanity has suffered for centuries under the burden of a collective negative, low-vibration energy that we "miscreated" long ago and continue to perpetuate in our lives. She asserts that this is because we have forgotten our connection with the Divine and with our own creative powers. Until we remember our connection to Divine Source and reclaim our innate Divinity, she says, we will continue to cause needless suffering to ourselves and others.

It is by clearing our negative thought, feeling, and action energies—spiritual prescription #5—that we make room for this positive transformation. In this chapter, we will explore ways to go about clearing negative energy from your life. When you clear yourself of negative energy, you make room inside yourself to focus intently upon the present and the future that you want to create.

Some of the energy clearing techniques that we will present in this chapter are free of charge and available around the clock via the internet, so that you can clear your energy anytime you like. You *can* receive healing energy through your computer, since energy is not limited by physical barriers. The others are from CDs, books, or other resources, all of which are listed in the bibliography or website list at the end of the book.

The Pulse Technique by Jo Dunning and The Diamond Alignment by Jacqueline Joy are two of our favorite energy clearing techniques. Jo Dunning and Jacqueline Joy are gifted healers whose painful journeys led them to profound connections with Divine Source/God. Through their willingness to serve Divinity in whatever ways would help humankind, they were blessed with healing abilities that have reached thousands of people worldwide. Their respective healing and clearing techniques are easily accessible and require nothing of you except that you be present and open to receive the energy.

Other powerful energy healing techniques we'll also share with you include The Violet Flame, Ho'oponopono, and the Healing Code.

Before Using an Energy Technique

The first step in clearing your energy is to make sure that you are working with your own energy. It seems odd for us to say that, but the reality is that we sometimes take on other people's energy without knowing it. This happens most often when we are trying to help someone who is in pain. Usually there is an exchange of energy, wherein we take on their negative energy and give them our positive energy. As a result, we feel depleted and are plagued by negative emotions that seem to come from nowhere.

Here's a simple way to clear yourself of this "foreign" energy:

> The first thing to do is to simply ask God or the Divine to send energy that is not your own back to the spirit guides of the people to whom it belongs. You don't even have to know whose energy you are carrying; just ask that it be sent back to their spirit guides. Then ask that your own energy be returned to you, cleaned and ready for you to use. It's as simple as that. When you have finished with that, imagine golden cosmic energy coming down through the top of your head and filling you up with supportive, neutral energy.

We suggest that you use this process as the first step for each of the additional energy clearing techniques in this chapter. It will also be helpful to consciously remind yourself to resist taking on their pain when you are trying to support someone who is hurting. Instead, express your care and concern for them while you envision yourself bathed in golden or white light. You can also refer back to Chapter Seven to the section on Grounding.

The Pulse Technique

The Pulse technique, developed by Jo Dunning, is a highly effective method of clearing negative energy from your life. Both of us use it regularly, and every time we do we are surprised by its power. Here is Jo's personal story of profound transformation:

> Jo was a high school teacher whose life was grounded in her spirituality. Her relationship with the Divine was her center, and she studied spirituality in depth. Jo cherished her connection with the Divine.
>
> She wanted to deepen that connection even further, and she prayed without ceasing to do so. Jo asked God to do whatever was necessary to move her to the next level of consciousness. Somehow, Jo knew that she would be able to handle whatever came her way as a result of her request.
>
> Several months later, Jo was brutally assaulted and left for dead during a home invasion. Her friend, who was also there, was killed. In the aftermath of that horror, Jo held firm to two unshakable beliefs: that this tragedy was for her highest good, and that she had within her all of the guidance and wisdom she would need in order to heal. She focused all of her attention inward, and asked herself with each new moment, "What is the next step I should take in order to heal?"
>
> This tragedy would not define her as a victim. In fact, Jo knew that her life would be better for having endured this trauma. She

didn't know how, and she didn't know when, but she believed it and kept it as her guiding mantra.

Sometime later, Jo began to manifest healing abilities that she had not previously had. She could lay hands upon someone and their pain would disappear. She could "see" through someone's skin to their internal organs and bones.

All of these abilities came as a shock to her; Jo had never wanted to be a healer. Nonetheless, news of her abilities began to spread. People started coming to her for help. Over time, Jo became internationally known as a transformational healer and speaker. Her life *is* better that it ever was, just as she had believed it would be, and she has worked miracles in the lives of thousands of people.

One such person, a nurse who was an early practitioner of The Pulse, offered The Pulse to a forty-year-old man who was dying of cancer. She did the technique for fifteen minutes with him. The man underwent scheduled medical testing the next day, and when she returned to work she was told that, to the amazement of his medical team, those tests had revealed no sign of cancer. He was in full remission. (You can find the complete story on Jo Dunning's website, http://www.jodunning.com.)

This story illustrates the power of The Pulse, and it is not the only instance of miraculous healing after using the technique. Deb Cummings, who is Jo Dunning's business manager, experienced such healing with The Pulse, and she generously agreed to share her story with us.

"It was pure misery." That was how Deb Cummings described the life she used to lead, one in which she hid her true feelings and eventually became completely housebound by crippling anxiety and panic attacks. Deb grew up in an abusive family, with an alcoholic father and a mother who was also a victim of the situation. She tried to put on a happy face, and strove to be perfect. It was the only way she knew how to make it through each day.

By the time she reached her late twenties, Deb was still struggling with life. She had had children, was a step-parent, and was still having frequent panic attacks. She was on several medications for both depression and anxiety, and carried a timer with her to know when the next dose was due. But sometimes the anxiety still broke through, despite her medication.

Eventually she suffered a complete nervous breakdown. Although she had somehow managed to keep working until that point, her therapist told her she must either stop working or be hospitalized. Her anxiety and depression had become so severe that she could not even leave her bedroom. Every aspect of her life was falling apart.

Sometime during this crisis period, Deb heard about a church that interested her. She felt compelled to check it out, and somehow managed to get herself to some services there. During one service, a woman named Jo Dunning was to speak about energy healing. Deb did not believe in anything related to energy work, and felt somewhat uncomfortable. However, she was equally uncomfortable walking out of the service, so she stayed through the hour. She could tell that Jo really believed in what she was saying, and that fact resonated with Deb.

As she left the service that night, Deb experienced the "presence of happiness," something she had never felt before in her life. The church asked Jo to return the next night to offer another energy healing. Despite her initial discomfort, Deb decided to return the next evening.

Deb signed up for Jo's email list, and one day she received an announcement for an upcoming training workshop in which Jo would teach attendees how to perform energy clearing and healing using her method, the Pulse Technique. Deb had no idea why, but she *knew* she had to attend. She signed up for the training. Then she got physically ill and developed intense back pain. Her anxiety skyrocketed. Still, she went.

Deb imagined all sorts of cult-like activities that might occur at this workshop. She decided that she would park her car in a spot that would enable her to leave if she needed to do so. When she got there, though, she found out that she had to leave her car at the base of a mountain and take a shuttle bus up to the retreat center. She feared the absolute worst. And still, she went.

Everything in Deb Cumming's life changed with this decision. Her marriage, her relationships with her children, her finances, her perspective on life, her sense of purpose and direction—everything. She describes feeling a huge shift in self-esteem and a true sense of inner peace. Within six months she was off all of her medications and had begun to practice energy healing. She offered energy sessions to anyone who was willing to receive them. She could not get enough energy—either receiving it or giving it.

Months later, Deb fell while at a restaurant. Her leg was injured, and in order to walk she had to drag the injured leg. Soon after the injury, Deb was performing energy healing on a client when she began to experience an influx of intense energy in her leg. Afterward, she was once again able to walk normally and without pain.

In another instance, Deb was in excruciating pain due to nerve damage she had suffered in an accident. Again, she was working with a client, this time by telephone. She had to keep moving to tolerate the pain, so she was pacing back and forth while on the call. Suddenly, she was flooded with the feeling of gratitude—a *deep* state of gratitude—and then the pain was gone. She believes that the nerve damage was a gift to her, so that she would be allowed to experience a miracle. She believes that everything that happens to us in our lives contains some sort of gift.

From her experience with Jo Dunning's work, Deb has developed a deep compassion for her family, and no longer feels pain, sadness, or anger when she recalls her childhood. Everything in her life has transformed, and she views life from a perspective of trust and love. She continues to witness miracles in her life and believes that "every single possibility in life is available." She is currently a coach and the business manager for Jo Dunning, as well as an independent practitioner of The Pulse and other forms of energy work that she learned with Jo.

You can experience it for yourself by doing an internet search on The Pulse Technique. There, you will find a short video featuring Deb Cummings, who conducts a free energy clearing using The Pulse. A complete clearing takes about six minutes. It is remarkably effective, and both of us use it on those days when we just can't seem to get out from under our negative thoughts and emotions.

The Diamond Alignment

Jacqueline Joy is another internationally known transformational healer. Her energy technique, The Diamond Alignment, came to her following a harrowing life crisis. Here is her story:

> Jacqueline Joy had been living a fast-paced life. She was married and had four children, a business, and an active social calendar, when one day she suddenly collapsed to the floor, unconscious. Over the next year, her life as she had known it completely fell apart. She had frequent panic attacks and endured the arduous and painful process of a divorce.
>
> Each day she would walk outside to her special place, a fallen oak tree, and lie down upon it. She would surrender to the energy of the tree and pour her troubles into the earth. She prayed for help, for answers, for relief from her pain—and somehow her pain was always relieved. She would later realize that her body was receiving Divine Energy Infusions and being rewired to carry the higher frequencies that would be necessary for her to sustain this healing energy.
>
> Over time she realized that this cosmic energy was bringing her into alignment with the profound peace and courage of her soul. However, each time she re-entered her life at home, she could not maintain her equanimity. Again, she turned to the Divine for help. She called for a way to sustain the courage, peace, strength, and joy that she experienced at her oak tree.
>
> Again, her call to the Divine was answered. Energy transmissions of light and color, "a divine Architectural Blueprint for a physical, yet invisible, Magenta Pyramid chamber that held the Cosmic Energy of Love, Joy and Wisdom" was transmitted

> to her. This Magenta Pyramid transmitted extremely high-frequency Spiritual Energy. As Jacqueline healed and became able to maintain her alignment with her soul through this Sacred Chamber, her soul's purpose was ignited. She was then guided to share this amazing experience with others who were seeking to align with their souls.
>
> When she began to share the Magenta Pyramid with others, she found that its energy frequency was too high for their bodies to experience comfortably. She then received the "design for a Green Pyramid Chamber, which harnessed Earth Energy and grounded the high frequency of the Magenta Energy. The two pyramids, joined at the base, now formed a Diamond Chamber that converted Cosmic Energy into Diamond Encrgy," which could be transmitted to individuals comfortably.

Over the past ten years she has slowly and carefully developed an online program that offers people around the world the opportunity to access the Diamond Chamber and to receive what she calls Divine Energy Transmissions, so that they can experience the peace within that comes from soul alignment. By using the Diamond Technology, you simply allow the Divine Energy Transmissions to fill you and support you.

Jacqueline's website, www.diamondalignment.com, makes this amazing technology available at all times of the day and night for people everywhere. The only thing you need to do is come to the site and say *yes* to the experience. It is not a religion or a belief system. Its total purpose is to raise your energy field to the highest possible vibrational level that is in alignment with your soul, allowing you to live in a state of inner peace and joy.

Jacqueline's soul mission is to create a "critical mass" shift in consciousness through the global delivery of the Diamond Energy Transmission. She is doing this through a worldwide Diamond Energy Grid that she has established across the planet over many years, which delivers the Diamond Energy Transmissions now to individuals in 198 countries.

We have recommended The Diamond Alignment to several friends and clients, and use it ourselves. For many who have experienced it, the technique has led to significant, positive life changes. Such was the case for Eleanor Smith, a South African woman who has used the Diamond Alignment in her own efforts to heal her life:

> The change in me has been enormous. Thirty days ago, I was a very anxious person who had just gone through a divorce after thirty-two years of marriage. The process took three years to complete. Having never lived on my own, I had to start looking for a new home, sort out my own affairs, and pay my own bills. Those tasks seemed very daunting, since in the past all such things had been taken care of for me. I was suffering from "inertia"—nothing could make me put one foot in front of the other. It felt as if life had come tumbling down around me, and I was fearful of the future. All of the "what if's" flashed by like a horror movie.
>
> After thirty days of using the Diamond Alignment, although I still suffer from immense fatigue, I'm celebrating being a free woman. I do my daily chores in a more spirited and lighter way. My cells are vibrating with Diamond Light. My body feels lighter. Everything seems lighter and brighter. I am filled with joy, my heart feels more open, I am contented and feel a deep inner peace. I actually love life! I am so grateful for this healing.

The Diamond Alignment requires absolutely nothing of you; you don't have to do anything, focus on anything, say anything. For this reason, it is a wonderful technique to use when you feel depleted and have nothing left to give. The process itself is soothing and relaxing. You can access The Diamond Alignment for free on Jacqueline Joy's website (see above), where you will also find some special Diamond Alignment packages that are offered for a fee.

The Violet Flame

Patricia Cota-Robles, to whom we referred earlier, offers another powerful energy clearing technique called The Violet Flame (*The Violet Flame CD*). Her work is based upon teachings she receives from Divine Source, or what she refers to as the "Beings of Light in the Realms of Illumined Truth." She has been receiving these teachings for several years, and shares them with others to help raise humanity's vibration.

The Violet Flame is a technique that invokes Divine energy to transmute "miscreated energy" into positive energy that she describes as "God's limitless perfection and abundance." It's a great technique to use when you find yourself thinking negative thoughts, having negative feelings, speaking or acting in negative or hurtful ways.

For example, if you notice one day that you are silently criticizing someone, you can use the Violet Flame to clear it by saying the following brief prayer:

Beloved I Am (God, or God within you),
I now invoke the Violet Flame
To transmute cause, core, effect, record and memory,
Every thought, feeling, word, or action I have ever expressed,
In any time frame or dimension,
Both known and unknown,
That reflects criticism or judgment
Of any kind.

This prayer effectively takes all of the energy of criticism or judgment that you have ever thought, spoken, or acted out, and transforms it into Divine energy of the highest vibration. You will notice that it also takes the emotional "umph" out of whatever thoughts or feelings you were having, and leaves you feeling calmer and more peaceful. You can apply the Violet Flame to any situation in which you are experiencing something negative. You can also use it to clear negative energy for all of humanity, using the same prayer or a shorter and simpler one, which goes like this:

> *Transmute, transmute, by Violet Fire,*
> *All causes and cores not of God's desire.*
> *I am a being of cause alone;*
> *That cause is Love, the sacred tone.*

This short verse serves as an excellent mantra that you can say at any time, in any place. And every time you say it, you are helping the entire world.

The Violet Flame CD is available for purchase through Patricia Cota-Robles' website, http://www.eraofpeace.org. It contains several prayers that both of us often listen to when we are driving. No matter what is going on in your life, saying a Violet Flame prayer is a great way to calm down and remember the big picture: that every "bad" situation provides a chance to clear your life of negativity! Patricia Cota-Robles knows that if enough people on the planet invoke the Violet Flame, we will reach a critical mass and that the earth and all life upon her will shift at once into the higher levels of vibration. It is her passionate desire for this to happen.

Ho'oponopono

Self I-Dentity Through Ho'oponopono is similar to the Violet Flame, in that its sole focus is the cleansing of negative energy in all its forms—our thoughts, memories, feelings, actions, even our archetypal ideas and patterns. This process is based upon an ancient Hawaiian Kahuna practice called *ho'oponopono*, the literal meaning of which is "to make right" or "to rectify an error" (*Zero Limits,* p. 5).

It is an ancient wisdom practice that allows you to let go of toxic energies within you so that Divinity can replace them with inspiration, the source of Divine thoughts, words, and actions. The original ho'oponopono process relies on a respected mediator to facilitate the actual cleansing of energy.

Self I-Dentity Through Ho'oponopono (SITH), on the other hand, is an updated method of the original ho'oponopono practice. It does not require a mediator; instead, you can practice it on yourself. According to Dr. Hew Len, Hawaiian psychologist and SITH teacher/practitioner, this updated version of ho'oponopono is a process of repentance, forgiveness, and transmutation of erroneous thoughts and behaviors into "perfect thoughts of LOVE."

SITH holds as its central premise that you are responsible for everything that turns up in your life. Everything. No exceptions. The idea is that if it is happening in your life, you created it, and therefore you must cleanse it. This includes all of your problems, illnesses, conflicts with others, and even the problems that the people in your life are experiencing … if it is happening, you created it and you have to cleanse it. As Dr. Hew Len provocatively asks, "Have you ever noticed that whenever you have a problem, you are there?" (*Zero Limits,* p. 41). That is, the common denominator among all of your problems is *you*.

According to SITH, then, if you want to heal yourself, others, or the world, you have to own the problem, apologize for it, and ask forgiveness for it. In so doing, the problem and its negative energy are transmuted into Divine energy, and healing occurs.

Most of us object strongly to the notion that we are responsible for everything, especially when things happen *to* us. We have a hard time seeing how we can be responsible for war, poverty, or famine happening half-way around the world. But the reality is that if we are all connected, then we all contribute to the world's problems and we are all responsible to fix them.

Self I-Dentity Through Ho'oponopono is a very simple process, using four short statements. You say these statements silently to yourself and direct them to Divine Source. You can also silently direct them toward people if the situation involves them. These statements are:

1. I love you.
2. I'm sorry.
3. Please forgive me.
4. Thank you.

You can use ho'oponopono for virtually any situation. For example, if you are in conflict with someone in your life, you can bring that person to your mind and say, "I love you. I am sorry for the pain I have caused you. Please forgive me. Thank you." It does not matter who is right or who is wrong. What matters is that it is happening, and the negative energy of it must be cleansed in order for healing to occur.

Dr. Hew Len actually uses the process to cleanse conference rooms and buildings where he is staying or working. He treats them as "living" spaces that have suffered from negative energy that people have left in them over the years. He apologizes to them and asks forgiveness, so that they can be filled with positive energy and love.

Dr. Hew Len once worked in a mental health unit that housed people with severe mental illness. Staff morale in the unit was very low, and employee turnover rates were extremely high. Patients were sometimes violent toward staff; in short, everyone in the unit was unhappy and the work environment was miserable.

Dr. Hew Len joined the staff and began to heal the unit by taking responsibility for all the problems there and then working on himself. He did not even meet with the patients in person! Instead, he reviewed patients' charts and used Self I-Dentity Through Ho'oponopono to cleanse their problems within himself. He cleansed himself on behalf of the staff, and even on behalf of the hospital building, which he saw as having suffered from the pain on the unit within its walls.

Working in this way, Dr. Hew Len achieved amazing results. Patients' mental health issues were greatly improved or completely resolved. Staff morale improved, and employee turnover stopped. The story is chronicled in an article entitled, "Self I-Dentity Through Ho'oponopono: Being 100 Percent Responsible for the Problems of My Clients," by Ihaleakala Hew Len, PhD, and Charles Brown, LMT. This article was reprinted in *Zero Limits* (see Resources).

Master healers and teachers say that ho'oponopono is one of the primary techniques they use in their own lives and with their students. Both of us have also used it often, and find it very effective in clearing negative thoughts and feelings. When you use it, you will find that it is quite emotionally and physically soothing. It opens your heart, and leaves you feeling more compassionate and loving.

Marci Shimoff, well-known teacher, international speaker, and *New York Times* bestselling author or co-author of numerous spiritually oriented books (*Love for No Reason, Chicken Soup for the Woman's Soul,* and *Happy for No Reason*) shared with us her personal experience using ho'oponopono. Her story illustrates the transformational and heart opening power of forgiveness:

> A very dear friend of mine, Tracy, had become angry toward me for something and had stopped talking to me. I was feeling indignant: I didn't think I'd done anything wrong, and I felt I was being misunderstood and mistreated. After a few months of receiving the "silent treatment" from her, I was scheduled to get together with a group of friends in order to help one of them move to a new apartment. Tracy was also going to be there, and I was worried that the silence between us would be really uncomfortable. We were going to be working together in our friend's small apartment, and I had resolved that I was not going to be the one to break the ice. After all, I thought I was the one being "wronged" by her treatment of me.
>
> Sure enough, we got off to an awkward start that day. After two hours, both of us were still being silent ice queens, so I left for a few minutes to go sit in my car. I was feeling angry, hurt, and discouraged. For some reason, at that moment I thought of Nelson Mandela—the hardships he had endured at the hands

of his captors, and how he'd been able to feel compassion and forgiveness for them. I thought, "If he was able to love and forgive in the face of prison hardship and beatings, I can certainly love and forgive in this situation."

So I sat in my car and practiced ho'oponopono, sending forgiveness and love to Tracy and also towards myself. After about ten minutes of silently repeating "I'm sorry, please forgive me, thank you, I love you," my heart softened, and I realized that Tracy wasn't mad at me just because of what had happened a few months earlier. I could also see ways in which I'd caused her pain over the years of our friendship. I began to feel deep compassion for her, and my resentment just dissolved.

I went back into the apartment feeling openness and love towards Tracy, but I didn't say anything to her or anyone else. Within a few minutes of my return, Tracy came over to me out of the blue and said, "Let's go unpack the boxes in the kitchen together." I was shocked; I hadn't said anything to her and yet she was treating me as though there hadn't been a problem.

A little while later at lunch, she offered me her fresh mango slices, even though I knew that she loved fresh mango. She then said to me, "Marci, I know you like these, so have mine." The energy change between us was dramatic—it was like night and day.

Later I pulled aside another friend, who'd witnessed the whole thing, and asked her what she'd said to Tracy while I was gone to change her behavior. She said, "Marci, nobody said anything to Tracy. What did you do?"

Forgiveness had unblocked both of our hearts, and had freed us both to give again.

And thank goodness things unfolded as they did between us. The friend we had helped move passed away less than a year after that incident. Once again, Tracy and I were back at our friend's apartment—only this time we were clearing out those same kitchen cabinets that we'd set up together. I hate to think what it would have been like if I'd held on to my anger and resentment. Life's too short to keep our hearts closed.

HeartMath

The Institute of HeartMath (http://www.HeartMath.org) is a very useful resource that offers tools and techniques to help you cope when you are feeling overwhelmed or stressed. Using the powerful energy of your heart, their techniques help you to change your negative emotion into positive energy. They also promote relaxation, so that your body can move out of its stressed state of "high alert."

People at the Institute of HeartMath have conducted a great deal of scientific research about the heart and its energy. One of their findings is that the power of energy from your heart is much, much greater than the energy from your brain. What you send out from your heart will have the greatest impact on the world and the people around you.

On the HeartMath site you can find a free tool called "Notice and Ease." This tool guides you through a short (about three-and-a-half minutes) process that soothes emotional distress. The "emWave" is also offered there, a small biofeedback device created by the Institute that measures your current stress or anxiety level and then assists you in achieving and maintaining a calm, peaceful state. We have both used it and found it to be accurate, fast, and effective.

When you experience negative emotions, your heart rate is altered and is no longer balanced with your brain or your nervous system. This imbalance negatively affects your health, brain function, and your sense of well-being. The emWave provides immediate feedback to you about your emotional state, and you learn the subtle changes in your thinking and your body that help to bring your heart rhythm back into sync.

As you practice this, you are able to bring about the positive emotional state more and more quickly. It is worth the price for how well it works.

The Healing Code

When we were nearing the end of the first draft of our book, we learned of a technique known as The Healing Code. Deb, a friend from Australia, had used it to help heal an infant who was dying. As Deb told the story, her friend had given birth to an infant who was gravely ill and rapidly declining. Deb rushed to the hospital to use The Healing Code technique on the baby, and she taught the technique to the mother as well. Within one hour the baby's condition had improved dramatically, and the baby went on to fully recover. When we heard Deb's miraculous story, we felt compelled to include this healing tool in our book.

The Healing Code was developed by Dr. Alexander Loyd, who had searched for years to find a way to help heal his wife's severe depression. He prayed fervently for guidance, and his prayers were answered when he was suddenly given the idea for The Healing Code. It was akin to downloading a file, only this one just appeared in its entirety in Dr. Loyd's mind.

He was able to see the entire process in his mind, and he wrote it down as quickly and completely as he could. He then immediately tried the technique on his wife. Within one hour, his wife's depressive symptoms were gone. He continued to perform The Healing Code on his wife for about three weeks, and her symptoms did not return.

On the heels of Dr. Loyd's success with The Healing Code, Ben Johnson was diagnosed with Lou Gehrig's disease. As a medical and osteopathic physician, Dr. Johnson knew that this disease had no known cure and was considered to be a terminal disease. He decided to try The Healing Code in an effort to heal himself. He used the technique every day for three months, and his disease completely disappeared. Dr. Johnson and Dr. Loyd have since dedicated their lives to helping people heal their emotional and physical illnesses completely and rapidly. We highly recommend their book, *The Healing Code: 6 Minutes to Heal the Source of Your Health, Success, or Relationship Issue.*

Below you will find simple instructions for using The Healing Code. They ask you to use a Truth Focus Statement while doing the Code, which is simply an affirmative statement such as "I am lovable" or "Nothing has power over me unless I allow it" or "I choose to forgive myself and others now." Create a statement that, although it may not feel true at the moment, you believe can be true with the help of the Divine. We suggest that you read the book for a more detailed explanation of this amazing healing tool. And when you purchase the book, you will have access to the authors' list of sample Truth Focus Statements.

Do the Code in a quiet, private, place where you can relax without distractions or interruptions.

Here's the sequence:

1. Rate the issue in terms of how much it bothers you, 0-10, 10 being most painful.
2. Identify the feelings and/or unhealthy beliefs related to your issue.
3. *Memory Finder:* Think back if there was another time in your life when you felt the same way, even if the circumstances were very different. We're looking for the same kind of feeling. Don't do a lot of digging—just take a moment to ask yourself if there was another time in your life when you felt the same way you're feeling now. We're going for similarities in the feeling, not the circumstances. If you're feeling anxious about an upcoming medical test, you want to ask if you have ever felt that same kind of anxiety when you were younger, not whether you ever faced a medical test before. Go for the earliest memory that surfaces, and focus on healing that first.
4. Rate that earlier memory, 0-10. There may be others. Look for the strongest or earliest, and work on that first. What bothers us now tends to be troublesome precisely because it's attached to or triggered by an unhealed memory. Often when you heal the earlier or strongest memory, all other memories "attached" to that core memory heal at the same time.
5. Say the prayer for healing, inserting all the issues you uncovered ("my memory as a four-year-old, my fear issue, my headaches," or whatever).

"I pray that all known and unknown negative images, unhealthy beliefs, destructive cellular memories, and all physical issues related to ________________ [your problem or issues] would be found, opened and healed by filling me with the light, life and love of God. I also pray that the effectiveness of this healing be increased by 100 times or more." (This tells the body to make the healing a priority.)

6. Do The Healing Code holding each position for around 30 seconds, repeating a Truth Focus Statement that counters any unhealthy belief, or one that addresses your issue. When you do a Healing Code, you don't focus on the negative, but the positive. Make sure you rotate through all four positions before quitting (usually several sequences). **Do the Code sequence for at least 6 minutes.** Make sure you go through all four positions before you stop. You can always take a little longer, especially if you rated your issue above a 5 or 6. We suggest 6 minutes as the minimum.

(First Position) Bridge: In between the bridge of the nose and the middle of the eyebrow, if the eyebrows were grown together.

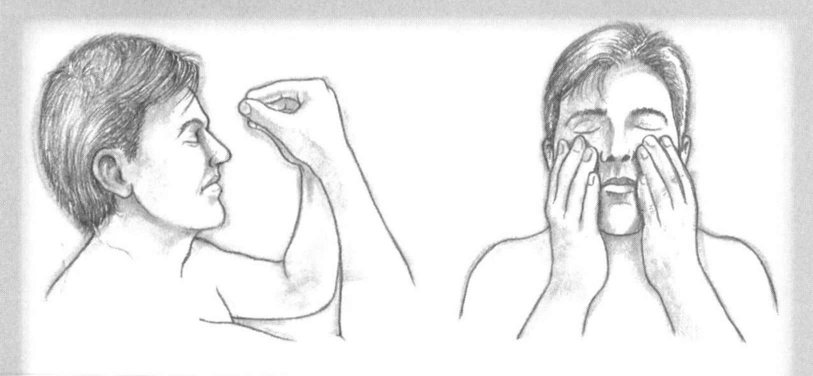

Main Bridge position Resting

(Second Position) Adam's Apple: Directly over the Adam's apple.

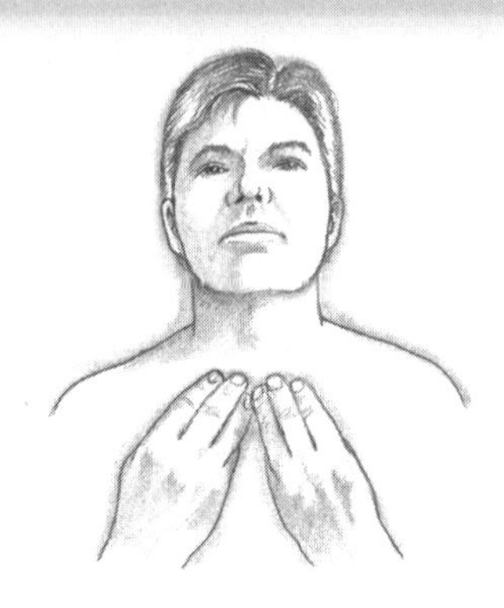

(Third Position) Jaws: On the bottom back corner of the jawbone, on both sides of the head.

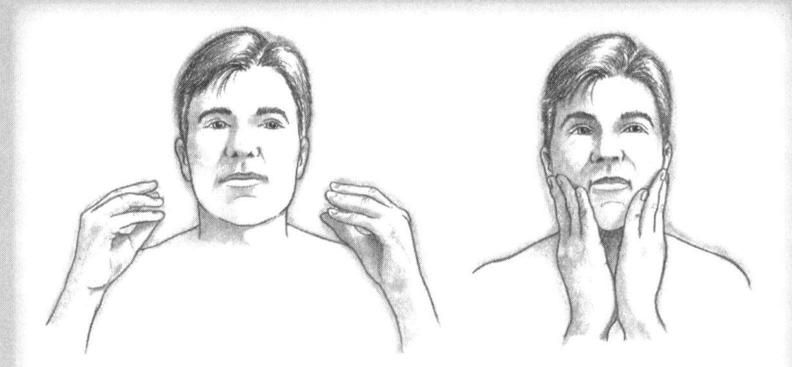

Jaws position

Resting

(Fourth Position) Temples: One-half inch above the temple, and one-half inch toward the back of the head, on both sides of the head.

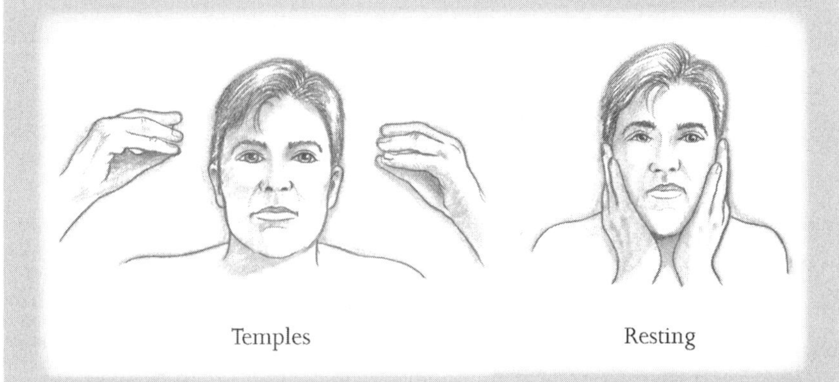

Temples Resting

7. After doing the Codes, rate your issue again. When that earliest/strongest memory is down to 0 or 1, you can go on to the next memory or issue that bothers you the most.

The Effects and Benefits of Energy Clearing

People experience energy clearing techniques in different ways. Some people feel an immediate shift in energy as they are using the techniques or soon afterward. Others don't feel anything noticeable at first, and later notice that their thoughts, feelings, and energy have gradually become more positive. In all cases, the clearing continues even after the technique itself is finished.

Using these techniques on a regular—or even daily—basis allows you to focus on creating the life you want. And each time you clear your own negative energy, you also clear it throughout the Universe!

10

Prescription #6:
Practice Forgiveness, Trust, and Gratitude

In addition to the techniques we have shown you for clearing negative energy, there are three other practices that can transform your energy—and your life. They are forgiveness, gratitude, and trust in your Higher Power—spiritual prescription #6.

Forgiveness and gratitude are powerful, high-vibration energies that can transform negative thoughts and emotions into positive energy. To forgive someone is to recognize that their soul is sacred and holy, despite whatever "wrongs" they may have committed. To forgive yourself is to recognize that same sacredness and holiness in yourself. We are all Divine beings, no exceptions.

Forgiveness recognizes that we are all following a spiritual path. That path includes the painful or upsetting things that people may have done to us in the past. It also includes the times when we have wounded others, intentionally or not. When we realize this, it is easier to forgive, because we can see that it has all been for our highest good. We can even feel grateful for the painful lessons when we see how they serve us. And gratitude brings us inner peace.

Gratitude naturally arises from within when you know that you are on a spiritual path, and that everything that unfolds is for your benefit. Life feels easier when you aren't filled with negativity about things in the past or fear about what will happen in the future. You are able to be present, to notice the beauty in your life. When you are really "here" and fully inhabiting your life in the moment, you can even start to notice the basic things that you have taken for granted, such as the fact that you can breathe, hear, see, smell, and taste. You can feel grateful for your home, your food, your body, your partner, your pets, running water, sunshine ... the list could go on and on.

When you are feeling bad, though, it can be hard to think of things that you are grateful for. For this reason, we suggest that sometime when you are feeling happier, you sit down and make a list of all that you are grateful for. It will help you during those times when you feel deep pain.

When we are feeling overwhelmed and can't find our bearings, we can go into nature or into a quiet place to meditate or pray. In the quiet, we are able to calm our emotions and begin to reconnect to the Divinity that is within us and to the guidance that it offers. Trusting your connection with your Higher Power is a helpful practice that can remind you that you are not alone on your path. Listen to the voice inside of you that is your own Divinity, and trust that your life has meaning and purpose.

Forgiveness

Forgiveness is often misunderstood. People think that they are supposed to "forgive and forget," bypassing the pain caused by what or whomever they are forgiving. But that is not the case. To forgive does not mean to forget, or to pretend that nothing ever happened. It does mean being honest with yourself about what happened, how you felt (or feel) about it, and choosing to let go of the negative energy around it.

Holding onto anger or resentment only generates negative energy that is harmful to you. You are trapped in an endless cycle of remembering what happened, reacting to it all over again, and multiplying the amount of negative energy you are creating.

If the person you have not forgiven is you, the process is the same. The only difference is that you are angry and upset with yourself instead of someone else. You remind yourself all the time of what you think you did wrong, and this creates more and more negative energy.

The negative energy of resentment and anger is toxic to your body, too. The toxic energy can actually lead to physical illness. In her book *You Can Heal Your Life,* author Louise Hay links physical illnesses to negative thoughts and feelings. She says that the remedy is to use positive affirmations to change your thoughts, knowing that changing your thinking changes your physiology.

For those of you who might want some help with forgiveness, we recommend Brandon Bays' book *The Journey: A Practical Guide to Healing Your Life and Setting Yourself Free.* This book offers her process to help people to work through their difficulties with forgiveness. Brandon Bays used her process to heal a large tumor in her abdomen, which she believes she created to encapsulate an experience that had been too painful for her to face.

Her process involved an inner dialogue with everyone who was involved in the original trauma. Through that dialogue, she was able to say everything she needed to say to them, and to ask them questions that helped her to understand all she could about how and why the event had taken place. When she had learned all she could from them, she visualized the entire situation fading away. Her book explains the process more completely, and is a helpful tool to guide your own forgiveness work.

Cathy met Lindsay, Canada's "Happy Mother Coach" (http://www.happymothercoach.com), at a writer's conference. Below, Lindsay shares her story of the healing power of forgiveness:

> Our home was filled with stress when I was growing up—about money and work. Mum handled it fine; Dad reacted by being angry, sad, and withdrawn. He also became overweight as a result of the situation, despite my attempts to make him face up to what he was doing to himself and to us. Rather than changing his behavior, he grew more depressed and more overweight. I felt quite angry about the "victim" role he had adopted, and eventually distanced myself from him to avoid arguing with him anymore.

Some years later, I was about to give birth to my second son. The first had been a C-section, so I was relieved that my second son would be natural. However, his birth occurred so fast, and without the benefit of pain control, that I was in shock afterward. I would not hold my baby and did not feel a bond with him. I was more worried about being away from my first son.

Things did not improve when I took him home. He became a troubled baby, frequently ill. He wouldn't sleep, wouldn't eat; he was always in discomfort. I felt angry and frustrated toward him, and was on the verge of antidepressants at the end of his first eighteen months.

I decided to consult with a naturopath, a very spiritual and intuitive woman who also did craniosacral work and energy healing. I hoped that she could offer relief to both my son and me. As she treated my son, she told me that he had been manifesting physically all the symptoms that I was having emotionally! His discomfort mirrored my emotional discomfort. She thought that my healing, and his, would come with forgiveness—I needed to forgive my father, my son, and myself.

She led me through visualizations of our hearts opening. I sent unconditional love to my son, and understanding and compassion to my father and myself. My dad and I had both been coping with life the best we could; my son was just suffering from my symptoms!

Knowing all of this freed me to repair my relationships with my son and my father. And I was able to let go of my guilt for having been angry with my son. My son and I developed the bond that had been missing, and my dad actually started to address his health issues. He even began meditating, which opened his heart even further!

How do you come to forgiveness? First, think of forgiveness as letting go of the negative energy of resentment or self-blame. You still remember what happened and you can acknowledge that it caused you pain. Next, look for the lesson(s) that you have learned from it. Know that those lessons are either a part of your spiritual growth, the other person's growth, or both. Consider what may have led to your hurting someone or to them hurting you. Might it have been a bad day? Could it have been because they were struggling with a personal issue? Is it possible that you even misunderstood what they said or did? Had you or they just received bad news?

There are a thousand possible reasons for the things people do and say. It helps to consider that, like you, they are likely doing their best. We are all imperfect creatures, here to learn from our mistakes and our experiences.

Finally, recall that even if you can't see it, there is a spark of Divinity within them, just as there is in you. Recognizing this, set them free to pursue their own soul's path. Imagine the other person in a boat, and see yourself pushing the boat away from the shore and out to sea. Envision yourself waving as the boat moves farther and farther away, until it disappears from your view. Smile as you say to yourself, "It is done." Then turn away, knowing that you no longer carry the burden of that negative energy.

If you find it hard to let go, recite the Lovingkindness Prayer for yourself and for them. It will help you to feel compassion toward both of you, which makes it much easier to let go and forgive.

Ironically, forgiving ourselves is often harder than forgiving others. In her book *Dying to Be Me: My Journey from Cancer, to Near Death, to True Healing*, Anita Moorjani writes that her lack of self-forgiveness led to her developing cancer. The disease spread throughout her body, and she was dying. During a *thirty-hour* near-death experience, Anita concluded that her cancer was a manifestation of her own self-judgment. She had always felt that she wasn't good enough, but finally understood deep within herself that she was much more than good enough—she was magnificent! She was filled with unconditional love, and able to glimpse the beauty of her True Nature.

Anita knew that if she decided to return to her body, her cancer would be healed as a result of the unconditional love that filled her soul. Anita did return to her body, and five weeks later all signs of her cancer were gone.

Dr. Wayne Dyer is a well-known spiritual teacher who was diagnosed with leukemia. He believes that his illness was the physical manifestation of his anger and pain surrounding his divorce. Dr. Dyer understood his illness as an opportunity for forgiveness and healing. He worked to cultivate compassion and love toward those who had hurt him, and toward himself. He utilized the energetic healing and cleansing techniques that we have presented, and received remote healing from miracle healer John of God. His body no longer houses the toxic energy that supported his illness; consequently, he firmly believes and feels that he has been fully healed. He trusts his inner knowing, and he shows no further signs of the leukemia.

Trusting your Higher Power

Most people think of the Divine, or God, as being outside them. But as we have said throughout this book, the Divine is within all of us. Meditation or prayer puts you in touch with your inner Divinity. That is one of the reasons meditation and prayer are beneficial to you! The more you meditate or pray, the more you come to know and to trust your Divinity, your True Nature. Nurturing that connection can be the source of profound inner peace.

Your inner Divinity speaks to you through your intuition. If you listen to it, you find that you are always receiving support from the Divine. Knowing this is a great relief, and it can transform your life.

Deb Selway, PhD, Australian author of *Women of Spirit*, recounts her unexpected experience of connecting with the Universe in the story below:

> I had always been a bit of a weird kid. I'd look up into the stars at night from a young age and imagine other worlds, other beings, other entities out there, bigger, greater, and much more intriguing than me. I had always sensed that there was much more to life than met the eye.
>
> Then, after stumbling through just a couple of years of high school and starting work at fifteen years old, I fell hard into adolescence. Life didn't seem all that magical to me. I felt really

crappy about life and what it had to offer me. I struggled with my sexuality, and by the time I was twenty I had come to feel that life really wasn't worth living … that is, until I heard the kookaburra laugh.

Amongst all this adolescent angst some friends of mine invited me on a riverboat cruise on the Murray River in South Australia. We hired a houseboat, all six of us women, and off we chugged down the river for a five-day holiday. I was always a bit of an introvert in those days (hard to believe if you knew me now!), so I pretty much kept to myself. I'd sit on the back of the boat and daydream, wishing somehow that life could be just that bit happier, that bit more interesting—and a whole lot more fun.

One night, we tied up by the riverbank for the evening, just before dusk. The gang was preparing a hearty barbeque for us all, and I decided to take myself off for a walk down river. I eventually found myself a beautiful sandy beach where I lay down to rest. For some reason, on this particular evening, I thought of the emblem on one of my t-shirts—the Vitruvian Man by Leonardo De Vinci (the man in the middle of the circle and the square). As I thought of this image I moved my arms and legs out to touch the sides of my imaginary circle, and I asked the Universe: "If there is really something, someone, or anything out there, please give me a sign now, because I've just about had it with life on earth."

At that very instant, in that very moment, the kookaburra began its raucous laugh: "Ah ah, ha, ha, ha, kook, kook, kook, kook, kawwww, ah, ha, ha, ha, haaaaaaaaaa." And then, as if by magic, I felt my spirit (for want of a better word) merge with the laughter of that kookaburra and with the joy of the all-encompassing, all-embracing, all-vibrating energy of the Universe. On that evening the Universe and I became ONE. In that instant I knew it. In that instant, I experienced it. In that instant I felt pure unadulterated peace and joy.

Well, now, that's about as close as I can come to explaining to you the experience that set me on a path of spiritual investigation and my constant quest to embrace the ineffable. So you would think that from that day on, seeing I had that experience and I really GOT what life, the Universe, and everything was about, that everything would be hunky-dory for me from thereon in. Oh, my friends, but if it were all so easy.

Life has been somewhat of a bumpy ride for me since then, including wandering through a few spiritual dark alleys; experiencing disintegrated relationships; going through episodes of poverty, prosperity, and poverty again. And yet for all of that turmoil I wouldn't change a second of it. From my perspective, more than thirty years later, it was and is all worth it. My challenges are not over, not by a long shot, but nowadays, instead of always forgetting the kookaburra in my life, I continue to constantly remind myself of its joyous energy and presence.

I encourage you, regardless of your religious or spiritual backgrounds, to ask for your blessing from your God or the Universe and to know, without doubt, that it will be given. May you embrace your own kookaburra and allow the laughter and joy of this amazing Universe to fill your heart, your soul, and your life, just as the kookaburra filled mine.

P. S. Just before I sent this off to my beautiful friend and author Cathy Thomas, I asked the Universe if it was the right thing for me to share this story with you. Blow me down, not two seconds later, I heard the kookaburra's call from just outside my office window. "Kookkk kaaa ah ah ah, ha, ha, haaaaa!" Gotta love this amazing Universe!

There is great inner peace in the reconnection with your inner guidance. You live your life with ease, knowing that you have within you all the wisdom you will ever need. All you have to do is to be still and listen to it—and then follow it.

Maggie Dillon Katz, Canadian author of the upcoming book *Less Stress with the College Mess: Expert Advice On The College Search Process,* offers us another story about trust in yourself and the Divine:

Maggie Katz had always known she wanted to be a mother, but she worried that she would not be "good enough" as a parent. Her husband, Joe, was ambivalent about the idea of having children at all, so they were childless when they entered the Peace Corps together. Maggie was thirty-three years old.

They were sent to the Marshall Islands, where they lived on a tiny island, next door to an elementary school. Maggie and Joe found themselves surrounded by children everywhere they went. When they went on walks, the children would join them. When they were at home, the children looked in on them through the windows. When Maggie tried to carve out some quiet time, the children were there. She interacted with them, observed them, saw their energy and their resilience. And she felt comfortable with them. Her fears about being a mother began to disappear. She started to believe that she could be "good enough" as a parent.

Several months into their Peace Corps experience, they got word that Joe's mother was dying. They had to catch a flight home immediately if they were to make it before Joe's mother passed. The flight was long, though, and she was gone before they could get there.

During the funeral, Joe was crying—something Maggie had never seen him do before. Suddenly, Maggie felt a presence directly behind her head—she recognized right away that it was his mother. In amazement, she began to feel incredible warmth throughout her stomach and abdomen, and, at that moment, she knew—absolutely and without a doubt—that his mother had just brought their future child to meet her future parents.

Maggie was awestruck. Her intuition was confirmed when later that day Joe told her that he thought maybe they should consider having a child in the coming year.

When they returned to the Marshall Islands, Maggie thought to herself, "I know why I came here." She had gone there to overcome her fear of being a mother. "I will be good enough," she thought.

Sure enough, Maggie learned soon after that she was pregnant. She did not worry about possible complications during pregnancy, or whether the baby would be healthy. She trusted that this baby would be born into this world in perfect health and with the support of the Universe.

Since the island had no medical facilities, Maggie had to leave the island as soon as she learned she was pregnant. Joe stayed behind long enough to gather their belongings and say goodbye. He met with their dear friend Banep, who had come by their home daily to check that the fish they had caught were safe for them to eat.

Banep was very sad that they were leaving, but his spirits were brightened when Joe explained that Maggie was pregnant. A huge smile came over Banep's face when he heard this news, and he said, "It's because of us." "What do you mean?" Joe asked. Banep replied that the whole island had been praying for her to get pregnant. The Marshallese people believed that it was a great honor to be a mother, and they had felt bad that at age thirty-three, Maggie was still without a child.

When it came time for Maggie to deliver, she had to endure long hours of horrific back labor. Each contraction felt like her back was being broken in two. The pain was intense, and although her husband and the nurses tried to help her with breathing exercises and visualizations, she reached a point where she was considering dying to escape the pain. At that moment, Banep's smiling face filled her mind, and he guided her through to delivery.

Maggie trusted that the Universe had been guiding her through each step of this process. She believes that she was guided to the Marshall Islands to learn that she could be a good mother. She believes that Joe's recently deceased mother came to her with the energy of her unborn child, so that she could feel the beauty of her child. And she believes that Banep was truly there to walk her through that child's birth.

This is how the Divine works in your life. People mysteriously show up when you need them. Situations arise that help your inner desires to manifest. Your job is to be the infinite receiver, to listen, and to allow the gifts to flow to you. As Anita Moorjani puts it: "This energy (unconditional love) flows through me, surrounds me, and is indistinguishable from me. It is, in fact, who and what I truly am; trusting in it is simply trusting myself. Allowing it to guide me, protect me, and give me all that's needed for my ultimate happiness and well-being happens simply by being myself (*Dying to Be* Me, p. 128)."

Gratitude

Gratitude is a state of grace. Masaru Emoto's crystal photographs reveal that the most beautiful and radiant crystals are produced by the energy of gratitude. In *The Hidden Messsages in Water,* Emoto says that "What the world needs now is gratitude" (p. 81) in order to save the planet and ourselves.

We share with you below a very personal story from one of our closest friends. While we were writing this book, her father became extremely ill. Her story describes the many ways in which she felt gratitude in the midst of a very painful experience:

> When Tammy Wilkins, MD, got the call saying that her father was being taken to the hospital, she had a strong feeling that the situation was very serious. She quickly discovered that indeed, it was. Her father had pneumonia, and was in intensive care. Fearing the worst, she decided to pack her "funeral clothes." Filled with dread, Tammy and her husband drove to her hometown, where her father was in the hospital—the same one in which she had trained during medical school.
>
> When she arrived, she went directly to the ICU—she had done a med school rotation there ... although it was familiar, the unit now felt ominous. Most of the patients were in medically induced comas, the place eerily still except for the hums and beeps of medical equipment.
>
> As she rounded the corner and entered her father's room, the sight of him stopped Tammy in her tracks. Her father was a large man, six-two, thick and muscular. But the man she saw in the hospital bed appeared weak and vulnerable. He was dressed in a thin hospital gown, motionless, with a long ventilator tube stuck down his throat. Part of his face was covered with the tape that held the tube in place. He was not even covered with a blanket; his fever was so high that they had to pack him in ice much of the time.

A ventilator whooshed beside him, forcing air into his lungs in a measured cadence that made her uncomfortable; the pause between "breaths" felt too long, and made her want to scream at the machine, "Breathe, already! Breathe!" A screen next to her father's bed flashed his heart rate and blood pressure. An alarm blared to warn the medical staff that his oxygen saturation was too low. Tammy took it all in and then began to sob.

One day bled into another, and the sights and sounds faded in her awareness. The medical staff gave Tammy and her family regular updates about her father's condition, each one delivered with no eye contact and worded carefully so as not to instill or destroy hope. Still, their body language spoke volumes, and it was clear that the medical staff did not believe that her father would survive. Tammy saw her father's test results: they were terrible. The doctor in her knew that he was not going to make it.

Unlike the staff doctors, though, Tammy could not maintain emotional distance from this patient. She sought solace in the hospital's small chapel. There, she sat facing a stained glass window depicting two white doves against a cobalt blue sky, soaring upward, toward the heavens. Tammy closed her eyes, and she could feel the sun's warmth as it shone through the dove's wings, onto her face. She allowed herself to breathe, at last, and felt the presence of God in that small space. Peace settled over her, and she surrendered to the grief and uncertainty that had become her constant companions.

She thought that it would help if she could understand this entire situation from a larger perspective. She needed to know the spiritual meaning of it for her father, and for her. She called Gloria Hemsher, a psychic with whom she had worked in the past and whom she trusted.

Gloria told Tammy that her father was deciding whether or not to stay in this life, and that he had been exploring the process of transitioning out of his body. He had been visiting—and enjoying—the other side. He was not in his body, and therefore not in pain. She told Tammy that she did not think her father would choose to remain in this life.

Gloria also offered Tammy a way in which her soul could connect with and comfort her father. At first when Tammy tried this, she could only silently beg her father to stay with her. Later, she reminded herself that it had to be her father's decision to stay or leave, and that Gloria had said that asking him to stay could create negative karma for her father and for her. Tammy needed to ground herself. She needed to remain neutral.

Gloria instructed Tammy to talk with her father using an exercise called "God of the Heart,"* in which Tammy's higher power would speak telepathically to her father's higher power. As she did the exercise with her father, Tammy told him that the painful issues between them in the past were over, and she expressed to him her sorrow for any pain she had caused him. She told him what a big influence he had been in her life, and thanked him for being her constant cheerleader. She told him how much she loved him.

Tammy had achieved a spiritual connection with her father that would not have been possible without Gloria's guidance. She was filled with gratitude, and knew that whether her father decided to stay or leave, her relationship with him was forever changed.

Tammy's father hovered near death for three weeks, and during this time his soul came to Gloria asking for help. She asked Tammy's father's guides to move nearer to him, and she explained to him what was happening. She told him that he was the only one who could decide whether he wanted to come back. She explained that he had completed his work for this life and if he came back it would be for "extra credit."

When Gloria shared this with Tammy, she felt profoundly relieved and grateful. Tammy understood that even though her eyes saw the horrible image of someone suffering, her father was actually at peace, bathed in the enormous amount of love that

---

*God of the Heart is an exercise taught in Gloria's book with John Friedlander, *Basic Psychic Development: A User's Guide to Auras, Chakras & Clairvoyance* (see Resources).

> poured from those at his bedside. Gloria told her that her father was shocked to realize how much people cared about him.
>
> Tammy's father decided to live, and was told by his guides that he would be able to heal extremely—and to the doctors, inexplicably—quickly. No one could explain the speed with which he recovered. He had been allowed to see his life from the vantage point of the other side, and he was forever changed by the overwhelming love he had received while he was ill.
>
> Between him and Tammy, a deep connection had been forged and profound healing had occurred. She witnessed her father's increased connection to her son, delighted in watching them together. Every phone call between Tammy and her father became a source of joy, and a reminder of the miracles that had taken place—his recovery and their spiritual journey together. Now there was only love, and her limitless gratitude for the gifts of this experience.

Gratitude naturally flows from living in alignment with your highest self. If you are living in this way, gratitude becomes your way of life. As you reflect on all the things for which you are grateful, your life becomes joyful. Good things manifest in your life because your vibration is so high that you draw them to you! In this way, you raise your vibration and you radiate positive energy.

Use gratitude as your barometer. When you notice that you have not felt much appreciation lately, take a moment to really reflect on what you love and appreciate in your life, and let that energy fill you up. As you do that, you will ease back into alignment with your higher Self, and back into the beautiful energy of gratitude.

11

Prescription #7: Consider Psychic and Astrological Information

PSYCHICS AND ASTROLOGERS HAVE been around since time immemorial. Both have met with their share of skepticism; after all, we do tend to have a hard time accepting anything that is not scientifically measurable and observable. Maureen Caudill writes in *Suddenly Psychic: A Skeptic's Journey* that after "reading the scientific literature of paranormal phenomena, I realized that in spite of the debunkers' claims to the contrary, a ton of scientific, peer-reviewed, highly respectable evidence exists to support the reality of paranormal and psychic phenomena" (p. 10).

It is also the case that virtually anyone can claim to be psychic, and the same can be said for some who pose as astrologers. Nonetheless, our experiences and those of countless others attest to the accuracy of information that can be obtained from reputable psychics and astrologers. It is our experience that psychic and astrological information can support traditional therapy in fundamental ways.

In this chapter, we will explore astrology and psychic information—spiritual prescription #7. Both are tools that help you see your life from a much larger perspective. And both can shed light on your life's purpose.

Astrology is a sort of blueprint of your life. When we have referred our clients for astrological readings, they have discovered that the significant events of their lives had been predicted in their natal charts. Typically, we have referred clients for readings when they felt uncertain about their life paths. Their natal charts almost always confirmed that they were right on course, doing exactly what they were supposed to be doing.

We have recommended psychic readings for clients when they were experiencing something that seemed not to fit with their current life circumstances. If therapy had not been sufficiently helpful and the issue persisted, psychic readings were often the next step. For instance, if a client was having a fear that seemed to have no basis in this lifetime, and if that fear caused a lot of problems in their life, psychic information could usually help them (and us) to understand the problem and to heal it.

At times we have also suggested a psychic reading if a client was having an extreme or disproportionate reaction to someone or something in their life. For example, if a client felt intense anger or fear toward someone who had never given them reason to feel that way, a psychic reading might reveal that they were reacting to something from a past life rather than anything in this life.

Several of our clients sought psychic information due to unresolved issues with someone who had died. Psychic mediums could often establish contact with the deceased person's soul and then facilitate a conversation between them and the client. Akashic Record, past-life, and life-between-lives readings were useful for clients who had similar unresolved issues, or who wanted to learn about their life purpose.

Typically, clients who had psychic readings were able to move forward in therapy and in their lives at a much faster pace. Being able to understand their life experiences in the proper context enabled them to resolve the issues and questions that had been holding them back.

It is important to mention that astrology and psychic readings are not necessary for everyone, and we don't suggest them to our clients unless we believe they would be helpful and healing. However, some clients are curious and eager to explore aspects of their lives and past lives, and choose to seek readings on their own. In any case, astrological and psychic readings are fascinating, and they offer a wealth of information that enhances personal and spiritual exploration.

Astrology

The roots of astrology can be traced back to 4,000 BC or earlier. Greek, Egyptian, Indian, and other ancient civilizations used it to predict climatic conditions, births, and other major events. According to William W. Hewitt (*Astrology for Beginners*, 1997), astrology is the oldest empirical science in the world. Around 600 BC, early astrologers began to base their findings upon the alignment of Earth, other planets, and the stars at the time of one's birth. This is the most common version of astrology practiced today.

By looking at your birth in relation to planetary and stellar alignment, astrologers offer insights about the challenges you face, your strengths and weaknesses, your personality tendencies, and the probabilities for what will unfold throughout your life. In *Astrology For Beginners,* Hewitt says that astrology provides "intelligent information … on every aspect of a person's life from cradle to grave" (p. 16).

The movement of the earth and other planets in relation to the stars eventually led to the development of the signs of the zodiac, with which you are probably familiar to some extent. These signs are part of the information used by astrologers to predict and interpret many aspects of people's lives.

Although we have included it in this chapter with psychic information, astrology is based on mathematical calculations, not on extrasensory or psychic experiences. And while it can show you likely outcomes, you always retain your free will to determine exactly how your life will go.

When one of Cathy's clients was struggling to see the bigger picture of her painful life experiences, Cathy recommended that she consult with a spiritual astrologer. The client was willing, and the astrologer was able to help the client gain an understanding of her spiritual tasks in this life. Using the exact time, date, and place of the client's birth, the astrologer created the client's birth, or natal, chart. The astrologer addressed the "South Node" of her chart, which indicated what issues and energies the client needed to clear from her past (karmic issues).

She also looked at the "North Node" location, which clarified her life's spiritual work.

According to Pam Gallagher, certified professional astrologer and founder of the Midwest School of Astrology in Cincinnati, it takes about half of a person's life to complete their South Node work, at which point they begin to focus more intently on their spiritual work.

Having clarity about your life's spiritual goals can be tremendously freeing. One client of Cathy's had spent most of her life searching for her perfect career and feeling like a failure for not having already found it. At age sixty, she felt such despair about her life that she was contemplating suicide. Cathy suggested that she consider consulting with an astrologer so that she could understand her crisis in the context of the big picture of her life.

When she met with the astrologer, she learned that the focus for her North Node—her spiritual purpose—was to create and maintain relationships. She was not here to focus on finding a career, but rather to hone her ability to connect with others. She immediately recognized that this was what she *had* been doing for many years! The client felt immense relief. The tension left her body, and she realized that she had been following her life's path all along! The next several years of her life would be filled with joy, which she had never before.

There are different types of astrology, and one of them is Shamanic astrology. It is similar to Western astrology, but it considers the placement of Venus and Mars, the Sun and the Moon to be especially important in relation to your birth date and time. Yoga instructor and Reiki Master Healer Irena Miller recounts her experience with Shamanic astrology:

> Somewhere inside, I always recognized my tendency to sense others' pain and to feel it deeply. People often said to me, "Don't take things so personally." But it wasn't something that I could disconnect from. I didn't have a choice. When someone was hurt, I could feel the pain in my chest.
>
> This concerned me, because there is a history of depression in my family, and I didn't want to sink into a swamp of sadness as some family members had. Luckily, I was blessed with an

> incredible mother who knew how to find the joy that surpasses all understanding, and she taught me how to connect to this joy. This kept me from succumbing to that profound sadness.
>
> To accompany the depression in my family there was a tendency toward addiction. It lurked around in the dark corners, and my fear of it caused me to avoid anything that could be addictive. I wondered sometimes if I was missing out on some of the fun that those things seemed to provide. But my desire to live won out. Addiction felt connected to death.
>
> I longed to understand who I was, where I was coming from, and where I was meant to go. I sought the counsel of Lisa Michaels, a gifted healer and shamanic astrologer. She did a reading with me, where I discovered that my connection to others' feelings was part of my path. I learned that I would always feel deeply and empathically, but that I needed to channel the emotion through creative expression of some sort. I felt drawn to movement and dance, and found that through movement like belly dancing I could move all energy that was not serving me through and out of my body.
>
> My reading also revealed that my focus in this life was to be on spirituality, motherhood, and dancing. It finally made sense of my inability to be a big money-making success in the corporate world. My head had told me for years that I had to force myself to fit into Corporate America because it was the only path. But my heart wanted to stay home with my little ones and create and teach yoga, and this reading showed me that my heart was leading me to the very path I needed to follow.

Irena's reading validated her life path, as has been the case with clients for whom we have suggested astrology readings. Our clients have often been surprised, if not shocked, by the accuracy of the information that, deep within, they already knew. Astrology has confirmed and illuminated the paths they have followed, and those they would follow in the years to come. It has also helped them to view the patterns and issues in their lives from a much larger perspective.

Psychic Information

Psychic information comes in several different forms, which are dependent upon the "type" of psychic you choose to consult. Some psychics are clairvoyant and can "see" your past and aspects of your future. Others are mediums, who serve as messengers for spirits on the other side who want to communicate with someone here on earth. And some are channelers, who allow spirits from the other side to speak directly through them to offer needed information.

Psychic mediums provide us with a glimpse of life after death. The messages they bring to the living confirm that the soul survives the body's death. Perhaps you have heard of John Edwards or James Van Praagh. Both are famous mediums, and there are likely thousands of others around the world. They bring healing, reassurance, and closure to loved ones by facilitating contact between souls who have been separated by death. Psychologist Kathryn Ferner, PsyD, recounts below the story of such healing for one of her clients, who consulted with a medium:

> "He's done it," I thought to myself, a wave of relief washing over me as I stood in the door of my office waiting room. Alex, sitting comfortably in a marine blue office chair, radiated a kind of gentle sadness, like the soft rain of springtime. His sandy hair still fell into his eyes, shoulders slumped on his long and lanky frame, but his eyes were filled with softness instead of the despair of each prior visit. He'd done it.
>
> We looked at each other for a long moment, quietly measuring. I knew and he knew that I knew.
>
> "Well, come in and tell me about it," I said, as I turned for the consultation office. He smiled slightly and followed me in the door.
>
> When I first met Alex, he was a broken man. With three-day whiskers, unwashed hair, and pain clouding his blue eyes, he was a drowning man looking for a life ring before he went under the last time.

I was an experienced, trained, and good psychologist, with some confidence that I could help him recover from the near-deadly blow life had delivered. But I couldn't.

His story developed over time. A recent divorce, living alone in the country, and then his son living with him. "I loved that boy," he whispered, "and I failed him." Joey had shot and killed himself, with Alex's gun.

"I've always had guns," he defended. "Grew up with them. Learned at ten how to hunt, track, all the things a country boy learns. Never had a problem. Never gave it a thought. Then I went to work, and when I came back, he was gone. Dead." Tears covered his face, and despair ran through him like razor wire, shredding him with every thought. And with all my years of experience, training, and skills, I couldn't touch it.

He showed me pictures of Joey, bright, alive, and passionate. Active, an avid sailor. Well-liked by many. And now, dead. And I couldn't seem to budge the grief.

Finally, I knew that in spite of everything, I had no more tools in my bag. I had a lot of tools, and I had used them all. Meditation, spiritual work, medications, guided visualizations, traditional therapy, EMDR, and so on. And nothing helped.

I took my last ditch effort. "There's a woman I know. She's a psychic. And she can help you. I know she can." Now I was out on a tiny limb. He could complain that I was totally cracked and damaging to him and to the public. But he was my client, and I had to make every possible effort to bring healing, or we were going to lose him, too. There was no doubt in my mind that he wanted to join Joey. The self-blame was killing him.

"I hope you'll see her," I told him, as I gave him her name and number. "I have no idea of her fee."

Each week, as I walked into the waiting room, despair, dark eyes reflecting pools of darkness and hopelessness reflected back at me, surrounded by the shards of desperation. Then that day, he was sitting in peace, and I knew he'd seen her.

"Tell me about it."

"I couldn't believe anyone could do this. She didn't even know Joey's name. She said I was grieving for my son, who had killed himself. You didn't call her, did you?" I shook my head no, which he already knew.

"She told me that he'd had a kayaking accident while on a white water rafting trip two years ago. How would she know that? I don't understand, but she did. I said yes, and she said that Joey had ruptured his spleen, and I told her yes, he had. It was a terribly serious injury. He was always a daring boy, taking risks." I nodded as he talked on, eyes unfocused, seeing the interview with the psychic.

"She said it was a difficult time, and told me more about his injuries, and I told her, yes, that was true. What he didn't tell you, she continued, was that he also began hearing voices. The injury wounded him psychologically. He was frightened, and was afraid to tell anyone."

I watched Alex as he told me the story, sad but peaceful, nodding his head at each point, and looking up at me periodically to check my reaction. While confused by how she knew these things, he accepted the evidence she had presented, and the new information.

"He killed himself because of the voices," he finished, looking at me directly with clear eyes. "It wasn't because I had failed him as a father."

We had processed that repeatedly, but this time he understood it to be true. And true grieving replaced the unremitting despair of the previous weeks, months, and years. He was on the road to recovery.

I only saw him one more time. He could deal with normal grief. A strong man, he would be all right.

After he left, I pondered on the gift that that psychic had given Alex. He now had the peace of mind and the ability to move on. And I thought, I want to learn how to do that.

And so I did.

We have a responsibility to use these non-traditional avenues to bring healing to our clients when nothing else will. It's a part of the sacred work with which we have been entrusted to return health to our clients.

This story illustrates the powerful impact that information from the other side can have for a grieving survivor. This client broke through immobilizing guilt that had prevented him from moving forward. The medium was able to provide priceless information that the client likely could not have found elsewhere.

Psychics who channel bring messages from the other side, too, but they take it a step further. They are able to temporarily suspend their conscious awareness, so that souls from the other side can speak directly to people on earth by using the psychic's mind and their voice.

Julianna Kallas is a psychic who resides in Boston. She has been working as a psychic for over thirty years, has lectured throughout the country, and has been featured on several TV and radio talk shows. She recently helped the Boston Police Department solve a quadruple murder case, and was interviewed by TV's *Psychic Detectives*. Below, she tells the story of one of her clients, Justin:

> As healers, our job is to look beyond the seen into the unseen and help the client transform it. Such was the case with Justin. He came to me several years ago, mainly, I think, to disprove a psychic's credibility. After all, according to him, he had it all: a six-figure income, wonderful kids, a great wife, and a mistress on the side. For him, according to his rules, life was good. So what could I possibly tell him that would make things any better?
>
> To his utter amazement, I apparently told him quite the opposite (my readings are channeled, and I don't remember them; he called me later to explain). His ego, I said, was going to lead him to an utter breakdown of his life as he knew it, at about the age of forty-two. (He was then thirty-seven, so that was in another five years.) Because his perspective on life was so narcissistic, as was the way in which he viewed others, I told him there was nothing I could do to help him at the time. His ego wasn't ready to hear the words I had to say. "Call me when you are ready to listen," was my parting advice.
>
> Indeed, five years went by before I heard from Justin. As he would recount it to me years later, he literally was sitting in a corner of his room sobbing. His life was falling apart. All

of a sudden, he heard a voice saying: "You'll have a complete breakdown at the age of forty-two." Here he was at exactly the age of forty-two.

Who had said that to him? At first he couldn't remember. Was he just imagining it? Then it dawned on him that it had been a psychic he had seen at a corporate event. He couldn't remember my name or anything about what I had said, other than the message of the breakdown. So he called the organizer of the event, was given three names, and called each one until he found me. It was as if his inner voice was speaking to him. He knew somehow that through finding me, his life could be redirected.

I picked up the phone to hear Justin crying hysterically. "You said I would head for a fall, and I did. I didn't believe you when you gave me my reading. I just laughed it off and felt you were completely wrong. But you were so right, and I just don't know where to go. My wife left me, my kids hate me, my mistress broke up with me, and my business is near devastation. Can you help me? Can you PLEASE help me? I don't know where else to turn!"

Finally, I could tell that Justin was in a place to listen and truly absorb what I had to say. His ego had been broken, and he was speaking from his heart. He really wanted to be healed. This was the beginning of his emergence from "the dark night of the soul."

For several years, I worked closely with Justin. Because he had been so humbled, he was now open to using me as an "intuitive" life coach. He absorbed every message I gave him and promptly acted on it. He began reading spiritual books, most importantly *A Course in Miracles*, a channeled book based on the concepts of unconditional love and forgiveness. He began to see how narcissistic he had been and how he really didn't have a spiritual connection to the heart of others.

At my urging, he also went into therapy and began working on issues he had with his father, his inability to feel accepted, and his diagnosis of ADHD. He began to have dialogues with his kids instead of yelling at them. He started to meditate on a regular basis.

> When he had read *A Course in Miracles* cover to cover (it is over 1200 pages) and had done all 365 lessons in the back, he finally confided to me that he wanted to go to his former mistress's husband and ask for his forgiveness. To his credit, he did it in person, and it was extremely cathartic for both of them. This was a huge step for Justin. It helped him feel able to get on with his life, and his willingness to be humbled by this experience was evidence of his growth. I knew then that his healing was nearly complete.
>
> I'm happy to report that Justin is now in a healthy romantic relationship, and his relationships with his wife, his kids, and, just as importantly, himself, are greatly improved. Because his breakdown was so overwhelming, so too was his recovery. He was literally transformed, mentally, emotionally, physically, and spiritually. He calls me every year on the anniversary of his "transformation" and thanks me for helping him to become the loving person that he now is.

Esther Hicks has written about her early experiences with channeling in *Ask and It is Given*. In it, she shares that she was instructed from the other side to practice meditation and told that she would be a channel. She channels the collective consciousness known as Abraham, and offers international workshops at which audiences can ask questions of Abraham. Another gifted channel, Karin Lubin, channels the collective energies from a group of wise spirits known as Osiris.

Both Esther and Karin say that they feel deep joy and love when they channel these energies, and they channel with the confidence that only good can come from these communications. Below, Karin shares her own story of discovering her ability to channel, and the initial connection she had with Osiris:

> About ten years ago, I was walking through a bookstore when a particular book caught my eyes. I put it under my arm and checked out, never opening it. The book I chose was *Opening to Channel* by Sanaya Roman and Duane Packer. I had no idea

why I had zeroed in on it; I was a school principal and regular meditator, but certainly not into the psychic world.

Once I got home I soon found myself absorbed by what I was reading, and I could barely put it down. I wanted to learn more, so I continued to read about psychics and channeling.

I soon noticed a change in the quality of my meditations. They had become blissful, and I felt that some sort of presence or energy was with me as I meditated. I asked for information—who or what was this energy that I was experiencing?

The answer came to me as "Osiris." I understood that this was a name, and I learned that Osiris was the voice of a group of wise teachers from the other side. Osiris told me that their purpose was to bring into balance and harmony the masculine and feminine energies that existed within me and throughout the world.

When Osiris spoke to me, I tried at first to record the voice through automatic writing, allowing the words to flow through me and onto the page without editing or censoring them in any way. I didn't even know what I was writing—I just wrote what I heard the voice say. The words came in a torrent, so that eventually it became too difficult to write them.

I decided to try speaking the words aloud instead of writing them, and asked Osiris to speak to my husband through me as a sort of "test case." I did not know what was being said, only that I was talking extremely fast. I did not fully understand all that was happening to me, but I experienced Osiris' energy as loving and blissful. When Osiris was present, I felt rejuvenated.

Osiris guided me to channel information to a group of my friends, so I offered individual and group sessions for a few years to people who requested them. At one point, Osiris told me that I needed to stop doing outside sessions, and that I must focus instead upon myself. After a period of time, I was again encouraged to resume my channeling work with others.

Here is the story of a client of Karin's and her experience with an Osiris reading (please note that if Osiris ever expresses a health concern, the client is advised to seek medical attention in that area):

> When Cheryl went for her first reading with Osiris, she had a list of questions ready. She intended to find out about her current relationship and what her next career step should be. Before she ever mentioned her questions, however, Osiris told her that she needed to focus on her health in the coming year. It was not what she had expected to hear, and seemed to her an abrupt "about face."
>
> She left feeling a little bit disappointed, because her own questions had not really been addressed and she had not really been thinking about her health. When she thought about it, though, she had to admit that she had been struggling with her weight for years, and she had recently had foot surgery. Perhaps it would be wise for her to focus more on her health, she thought. Osiris had offered specific things for her to do, and she decided to take the messages to heart.
>
> Cheryl described this as her "good Divine shift." Soon after she met with Osiris, she attended a large event at which she was introduced to a woman who invited her to join her weight-loss program. It was as if this person had been brought to her to help her. And that was just the beginning of the synchronicities! In 2005 she had adopted as her mantra the saying "Choose Faith over Fear." After the Osiris reading she started to fully live out that mantra. It felt to her as if life began to present her with one positive opportunity after another. And all she needed to do was to say yes!
>
> Cheryl had always loved a song by Jana Stanfield, titled "If I Were Brave." Sometime after she had had her Osiris reading, she attended a brunch fundraiser. To her absolute astonishment, Jana Stanfield walked into the event. She was able to talk with Jana, told her about the singing lessons that she had been taking, and that she had chosen Jana's song to sing for her class. *Then*, Jana asked Cheryl to sing with her at the brunch!

> Although Cheryl was *terrified* of singing in public, she did it. The two went on to become good friends, and Cheryl's good fortune continued to unfold. The end result was that her health improved, but so did her relationships and her career. The questions that she had not been able to ask Osiris were nonetheless answered. She knew that there was a "Force greater than (she)," one that knew what she needed better than she did. It was very clear to her that she was being guided by that higher wisdom. To this day, she still marvels at how clear that message was.

We introduced you to our friend Irena in an earlier story. Her astrology reading two-and-a-half years earlier had told her that she would have another child. The following story recounts her reading with Osiris. When Irena initially called Karin to set the appointment, she was told that Osiris had said it was not the right time, and that she needed to schedule it for two weeks later. She had been forewarned that that could happen, but felt curious about it nonetheless.

During the waiting period, Irena's mother passed away. She realized that her appointment with Osiris was to take place after her mother's funeral, and quickly understood why Osiris had wanted her to wait. Here is what Osiris said:

> Irena was told by Osiris that the passing of her mother brought with it a great healing for Irena and for her family. Osiris encouraged her to stay grounded in her body—and Irena knew that she had been trying to connect with her mother in the spirit world. She was told that she was in a moment of transition and she should not do much outwardly. She was to feel into the transition and amazing beings would come into her life. (She was unsure if these were on the physical plane or spirits).
>
> They told her that things would be evident after eight months and it was important for her to say yes to what the Universe provided if she really loved it. She would find that her life would take a slightly different track than it was on at the moment.
>
> Osiris told Irena what many others have said, that she was a wise woman with the gift of sharing wisdom and knowledge

> from the heart. They saw her surrounded by the blue light that identified her as a "teacher," a wise spirit whose purpose was to teach others. They talked about how nurturing she was and how she operated from integrity. They said Irena was deeply connected to Spirit—the same information that had been given to her by her astrologer.
>
> The most astonishing part of her reading was that Osiris inquired about a third child (she only has two children), saying "What's up with the third child?" These were the *exact* words that Pam Gallagher had used over two years before.
>
> Irena says that logically it made no sense to have another child, and yet oddly, her four-year-old daughter had been talking a lot about her "little sister" lately. They thought she must be talking about a friend. Then at the bank, right *before* the reading, the bank teller asked her if she only had two children. He said something akin to, where is the other child? Are these your kids? Only two?
>
> After the reading she was clearing out her mother's drawers and came upon an unaddressed gift card that said, "It's a girl." Mind you, Osiris had said that her mom would be helping to bring this little one in. Osiris did say to her that she could say yes to the baby or that she wasn't ready.

Irena was willing to share this very personal story to illustrate that sometimes the information learned through a psychic or channeled reading can be difficult to take in. Irena needed to listen to her inner wisdom in order to decide how to proceed with the information given to her. She also wanted to let others know to listen to their intuition should they encounter a similar situation after a reading.

Irena noted that she was given the same information by two different readers who were strangers, separated by 1,500 miles. This fact made clear to her that she should take the information seriously. Although she has not yet decided what to do with what she learned, she is taking her time to listen within, and to pray for guidance. Free will is always at work in our lives on earth. Irena may have agreed prior to this life to bring in three children, but she is free to decide now whether or not to follow that path. She trusts that she will know what is in her highest good.

Osiris, like many other Spirit Masters from the other side, is able to see our human lives from the infinitely greater perspective of countless lifetimes across eons of time. Randy Crutcher, Karin Lubin's husband, was a psychotherapist when he received his first channeled reading many years prior to Karen becoming a channel. He shared with us that when he left that session, he felt as though he had just experienced "the equivalent of thirty psychotherapy sessions." He was awed by the ability of the psychic to help him see the bigger picture of his life.

The wisdom of these Spirit Masters is an invaluable gift, because it illuminates our soul's purpose and our earthly purpose. The challenges of our current life seem much less daunting in the context of that understanding.

The Akashic Record

The Akashic Record is the collection of all the information about all events that have ever taken place in history. It is like the unabridged dictionary of everything. In Kevin Todeschi's book *Edgar Cayce on the Akashic Records*, he quotes Edgar Cayce describing the Akashic Record in this way:

> Imagine having a computer system that keeps track of every event, thought, image or desire that had ever transpired in the earth. Imagine, as well, that rather than simply a compilation of written data and words, this system contains countless videotape film and pictures, providing the viewer with an eyewitness account of all that had ever happened within any historical time frame. Finally, imagine that this enormous database not only keeps track of the information from an objective perspective but also maintains the perspectives and emotions of every individual involved. As incredible as it may sound, this description gives a fairly accurate representation of the Akashic Record. (p. 2)

Cayce also said that people could tune into the Akashic Record just as a radio tunes into radio waves, and thus have access to the Record's contents. Cayce lived in the early 1900s, so knowledge of the Akashic Record is clearly not a new development.

In the context of Cathy's work with clients, she has sometimes suggested that a client seek an Akashic Record consultation. She has found it helpful when a client has been unable to make progress in therapy and no one on the treatment team could figure out the cause of the resistance. Akashic Record consultations are almost always tremendously helpful to the client, and to the treatment team. The client learns about past-life issues that have been impacting their current situations and impeding their progress. This knowledge enables them to understand and resolve the issues so that they can move forward.

The story below was written by Nikkea, the client of our colleague Sue Telintelo. Nikkea's Akashic Record reading led to a remarkable shift in her life. When we read Nikkea's story, we found it so inspiring that we could not bear to shorten it by much, for to do so would have robbed it of its full power. So we decided to share it with you nearly in its entirety. It shows the power and depth of the knowledge that can be gained in these readings:

> I decided to seek therapy after a terrifying period during which my two-year-old son, Jonathan, had developed a seizure/sleep disorder that doctors could not diagnose. He would awaken during the night to devastating episodes of uncontrolled twitching that took over his entire body. I knew that some part of him was aware of what was happening; his big blue eyes reflected intense fear, as though he was watching a scary movie. When the episodes ended, he would cry out, "Help!" and "Mom!"
>
> My husband and I were helpless to stop the episodes, and we had exhausted every medical option we could think of. Despite countless medical tests, doctors could not identify the problem and did not know how to treat it. In an effort to show the doctors what was happening, my husband and I monitored, observed, and videotaped the twitching episodes, feeling helpless and

confused. Everything felt so out of control in my life, and I felt I had nothing to grasp onto.

I had been very nervous when I was pregnant with my son and his twin sister. I was terrified of failing them, of not protecting them. Now my fears were coming true with this bizarre illness that had invaded my son. Then Jonathan and his twin sister, Ella, were born prematurely, and my son was not predicted to survive. I had felt panicked upon hearing that news, and I remember thinking, "Oh I can't lose him! What can I do to help him? I have to fix this!"

But the doctors told us we should tell him goodbye, because he likely would not survive the night. We told our tiny son that we loved him, were grateful he had shared a small part of his life with us, and that we trusted in his choice to stay on earth or to transition.

As I held him for the last few moments that night, his body pale and his fingers blue, I told him that I loved him so much, and that I believed in him. "I can't abandon him!" was my thought, as I felt my world crashing.

The next morning, the doctor said that our boy must have some powerful angels, because he pulled through and was continuing to improve. We were elated, of course. My mother, having no idea what had happened the night before, called when we got home to tell us about a dream she had had about Jonathan.

She told us, "I was walking with my brother Tom (who was deceased), and he led me to your house. We knocked on the front door and Jonathan answered, but he was already nine years old. He told me, "Nanny, I know what love is … because I see it all around me." I was amazed at the way Jonathan's soul had connected to my mom's, offering a message to us all that he had felt our love the night before, and had heard our words.

Several days later I had to take our daughter home and leave Jonathan behind. It was excruciating to leave him there as we took her home, even though I returned right away.

Back to the present. My husband and I had planned a trip to Mexico for our anniversary. I noticed that ever since we had booked the trip, I had had intense feelings of not wanting to fly on a plane—an extreme change from my childhood, when I had enjoyed plane rides. The thought of it made me ill, and caused a wave of fear to rush over me. I told him that I had changed my mind and I didn't think I could get on the plane.

My fear of planes had become incredibly intense during my pregnancy with the twins. I had previously had an anxiety attack during a flight, and had believed that we were going to crash as we flew through a large thunderstorm. My newly developed phobia of flying became the focus in my therapy. During a guided imagery exercise, I saw my plane going down. I was not afraid of dying or of the pain of a crash; it was the going down, descending toward the crash, that I feared most—the feeling of being out of control and helpless.

I recognized that fear of being out of control, needing desperately to help or to fix things. I had felt it when my son was ill, and I had also felt it during my pregnancy. I had been afraid then that I would fail as a mother, and I still felt like a constant failure as a mother. Actually, I could link my fear of failure and being out of control all the way back to childhood! It had always been a theme in my life.

My therapist, thinking that some of my fears might have past-life roots, suggested that I have an Akashic Record reading. I agreed, and made the appointment with a woman named Toby Evans.

The minute she began talking about my Akashic Record, I began to shake and my palms became very sweaty. My hands trembled, and my insides were quivering. I felt sick to my stomach, not realizing that my body was reacting to the memories. I resonated deeply with the information she offered.

Toby told me that in my past life, I had been an air force colonel named Nicholas. I had been overly responsible, overconfident, and believed that I could handle or fix anything. I had planned a flight for a day on which the weather conditions were not good for flying. Despite warnings from my fellow colonel (who she said is my husband in this life), I decided to go up anyway—with two young pilot trainees whom I loved like sons. Toby said she felt that these two souls were in my life in my present lifetime. She had no idea that I had children, let alone twins. Indeed they were in my current life, as my twins.

We encountered a bad storm and were flying through it when the plane began its nosedive. I could not get control of the plane, and I was totally disoriented by the dense cloud bank that surrounded the plane during its drastic plunge. There was nothing I could do—the controls were not working. I kept thinking, "If I could just see, I could get a sense of direction and I could fix this! I have to fix it!"

But I couldn't, and the plane crashed. Both young trainees were killed. I had failed them, failed to keep them safe. I had lost control. I could not leave them there, could not abandon them. Upon crashing, I had such an intense love and attachment to these boys and to my role on earth that a part of my soul remained, earthbound, in the form of Nicholas, stuck between this world and the next. He had been trying to get my attention for many lifetimes so that all of this could be brought full circle.

Until my session with Toby, I had ignored Nicholas and held fast to my desperate fear of losing control. But suddenly it all made sense. My fears of losing control, of failing as a mother, of desperation to help my ailing son (and then my failure to do so), my fear of flying, my terror of failing my children while I was pregnant … I had failed to protect my trainees in my last life, so how would I protect my own babies? My past life was bleeding into my current life and causing all of my fear.

All this had activated Jonathan's cellular memory of the crash and my terror of losing him again. His seizures were a symptom of this cellular memory.

My soul was pushing me to bring the all the pieces together. I needed the Akashic Record reading to bring my fears—of losing control, of losing my twins, and of flying—into the light. No amount of therapy, meditation, or guided imagery was going to achieve this. I also needed to understand my past lifetime and its connection to the issues in my present life, in order to forgive myself for what had occurred in both lifetimes. Now that it had come full circle, healing could finally occur.

Toby was also able to offer me tools to empower and assist me with the upcoming plane ride to Mexico. It would be an initiation of sorts, letting go of Nicholas and becoming more fully who I am.

The night after our session, I awoke suddenly, as though I could feel someone standing over me. Upon opening my eyes, I saw a male standing next to me, and I heard within me the words "Thank you." I recognized that it was the voice of the part of my soul that had been Nicholas in my previous life. I softly cried tears of joy upon hearing him, and knew together we had reached a new level. I was so grateful.

The trip to Mexico would be the first time that I had left my twins in someone else's care. It would also force me to confront my fear of flying. As we crossed the walkway to the plane, all I could feel was intense fear. Past-life memories flooded me: the flight in which my trainees had been killed was suddenly vivid in my mind.

I wanted all of it to just come up so that I could work with it, to access my emotions from that lifetime and allow them to move through me. I needed to feel in order to heal.

During the flight, I used the "sandbag" tool Toby had taught me. I let go of imaginary sandbags that contained all the ways in which I blamed myself, felt ashamed for the plane crash, and projected my fear and sadness onto others. I felt lighter upon landing, as though I had accomplished a major task by just *being* with my feelings.

The flight home was more intense. At the airport we were informed that we could not sit together, and I panicked. A few minutes later, I remembered that I was here to confront my fears. I told the people at the counter that I would be okay and that I could be without my husband. I had to *feel* it all once again, and surrender to the process, however it was to unfold.

The flight was incredibly bumpy because we flew through turbulence. Logically it was ridiculous to be upset or worried—I knew that the chances of the plane crashing were slim. But I also knew that I had to allow my feelings to be. I tried to fall asleep, but I couldn't. Waves of panic rushed over me like a waterfall. Descending in the plane was the hardest part, that sense of dropping through the sky that was so horribly familiar. We went through very thick clouds that seemed to go on forever. I couldn't see anything, which fueled my fear. But I trusted in the process, and knew I had to feel every aspect of this memory in order to forgive myself.

I knew that although I couldn't see through these clouds to the firm ground below me or the sun shining above, both were still there. These were the clouds that Nicholas could not see through, and that had caused him to lose direction as his plane descended rapidly. I knew there was nothing I could do, that it was not in my hands to control the plane. What *was* in my hands was the chance to use this sacred time to heal, and I was making the conscious choice to do so.

As soon as I began to release my control and my fear, I felt forgiveness toward myself. And at that moment, we came out of the clouds and I could see the ground. The timing was divine. I had needed to descend into the density of the clouds and the density of the fear in order for my spirit to ascend. I felt suddenly and blessedly free—from the fear, from the guilt, from the pattern of control.

I thought about my kids, waiting for me on the ground. They were Teachers, helping me to learn that there is no death and no ending—only love.

During my Akashic Reading, Toby had suggested that I talk to Jonathan's subconscious. I remembered our talking to him in the NICU the night we thought he was going to die, and I recalled my mom's dreams of Jon talking to her. I knew through those experiences that a part of him was always listening.

That night, as he lay sleeping, I told him that he was not to blame for the plane crash all those years before. I told him that this was a new lifetime and that he was safe and loved, and that we were together again.

Within one week, he stopped having seizures completely. The doctors were completely baffled. We witnessed the transformation of our precious little boy, from fearful and tormented to happy

> and thriving. He was, at last, free. He was smiling, feeling free. He is now our thriving little boy.

This story almost takes our breath away! We have read it several times, and it still gives us goose bumps. Nikkea used the knowledge she gained from her Akashic Record reading to heal her own divided soul and the souls of those she loved. Her son's mysterious illness disappeared when she shared with him the information that would set him free. She embraced her insecurities, her fear of failure, her guilt, her terror, and her panic, all the while trusting that her Higher Self would guide her—quite literally—through the clouds.

As alternative healing becomes more mainstream, clients are often the first to suggest that they include it in their therapy work. The same is true for psychic information. Bruce Lipton noted this in *The Biology of Belief*, saying: " … we are already in the midst of a very slow shift in medicine, propelled by consumers who are seeking out complementary medicine practitioners in record numbers. It's been a long time coming, but the quantum biological revolution is nigh. The medical establishment will eventually be dragged, half kicking and screaming, full force into the quantum revolution" (p. 121).

Sometimes, our clients have sought psychic or alternative healing on their own and then brought it to their therapy. They have taught us and spurred our exploration, at times gently pushing us more deeply into the psychic world than we intended to go. One client had been in despair, believing that she should be further along on her life path than she was. Hoping that it might provide some clarity, she sought a numerology report from Shaina Noll (the New Mexico therapist whom we mentioned in an earlier chapter).

The report proved to be the turning point in her life and in her therapy. It confirmed that her childhood had been extremely difficult and painful, and that this had been a part of her life plan. The second half of her life, however, was to be filled with joy and healing. All she had to do was to let it unfold. The client was able to shift out of her despair and into hope. She saw that she was right on schedule, doing exactly what she was supposed to be doing.

It can be a bit scary, at times, to refer our clients for psychic readings. While we both believe that the readings will be helpful, there is no way for us to know what our clients will be told or how they will react to the information. One client, for example, had been feeling chronically fatigued and unmotivated about her future. She had been unable to get better and wanted to understand what was causing her to feel that way. Cathy referred her for a past life reading, during which the psychic told her that a dead relative's spirit had been living inside her and draining her energy.

Cathy was quite upset when she heard this. She didn't believe at the time that someone else's spirit could live in one's body, and didn't know how her client would feel. The client, however, resonated with the information, believed it to be true, and felt relieved to learn it! More incredible still was the fact that the psychic was able to help the spirit's energy leave the client's body.

The client began to recover her energy almost immediately. Less than one week later, the client had found and enrolled in a graduate school program. She earned her master's degree at an accelerated pace, and wrote and published a book while studying for it. Now several years later, she reports that her energy remains full and vibrant, and she continues to thrive.

Psychic and astrological readings offer information that can transform people's lives. They can connect you with the infinite wisdom of the Divine, illuminate your life's purpose, and help you to understand events and experiences from a much larger perspective.

Part Three

The Bigger Picture

12

We Are Immortal Beings

In the last chapter, we introduced you to the Akashic Record and to the notion of past lives. Both of these concepts point to the fact that we do not really die at all, that there is life after life. They also imply that we live many lives, and that the purpose of these lives is to advance the growth of our souls.

The idea of spiritual evolution through many lifetimes may seem far-fetched to you. It may conflict with your religious beliefs, and this may cause you to dismiss the notion altogether. But if you are willing to consider the possibility, you may come to understand the true meaning of your existence: to help yourself and humanity move ever closer to Divine Source.

For now, just suppose that you *have* lived other lives prior to this one. And that it goes like this: at the end of each lifetime, your soul has separated from your body and you have entered another plane of existence. On this other side you have reunited with your ancestors, friends, and other people who compose your "soul group," the people with whom you have remained connected throughout your earthly sojourns.

Just imagine yourself in this heavenly realm, your "life after life," completely enveloped by unconditional love that is unlike anything you have experienced here on earth. It is so different from life on earth … yet it feels familiar to you. It feels like home!

Feel yourself light, freed from the density of human form, basking in the healing energy that now surrounds you. This is your time for rest and renewal, after the hard work of your life on earth. You are becoming ever more radiant as you are filled with Divine Love.

And envision yourself now entering, with the full support and unending love of your guides and angels, a peaceful chamber in which you can review the earthly life that you have left behind. This is not a tribunal in which your actions will be judged and you will be punished. Instead, you review the spiritual lessons that you faced in that lifetime, and your guides and elders help you to decide upon the lessons that you will carry forward into your next life. The tone is gentle, loving, free of judgment and criticism.

You linger in this heavenly realm for as long as you like. Then, when you are ready, you return to earth to begin the next phase of your soul's advancement.

That is the reason for living all these lifetimes: to face the challenges and experiences in each lifetime that will facilitate your spiritual growth. With each incarnation, your vibration raises to a higher level and you come closer and closer to the Divine.

When you view your life from this perspective, you are able to embrace your earthly trials and tribulations as opportunities to raise your vibration and advance your spiritual development. Each new lifetime offers you the chance to practice your co-creative powers; to consciously choose your thoughts, feelings, words, and actions to generate positive and loving energy.

Mind/body healing expert Deepak Chopra has been teaching for many years that our soul does not die when the body expires. That very word, *expires,* is an accurate description of physical death; your body reaches its expiration date and can no longer serve as a suitable earthly vehicle for your soul. At this point, your soul takes leave of your physical body and enters a different plane of existence.

It is a sort of transcendence, which Dr. Chopra explains in his book *Life After Death: The Burden of Proof*: "As much as we try to explain it, what happens when we die remains a miracle. We move from one world to another, we shed our old identity to experience 'I am,' the identity of the soul, and we assemble the ingredients of a completely unique life in our next body" (p. 267).

Both of us believe in reincarnation for the purpose of spiritual growth across lifetimes. Ideally, each life affords us the chance to meet and master the spiritual tasks that we have chosen for that lifetime. If we fail to learn our lessons satisfactorily—in our own eyes and in the loving eyes of our spiritual masters on the other side—then we usually choose to repeat those lessons in the next lifetime. Once a lesson is learned, we advance to the next task on our spiritual path, with the ultimate goal being our merger with Divine Source.

Life on earth is viewed on the other side as a very difficult way to learn soul lessons. In *Destiny of Souls,* Michael Newton, PhD, explains that clients have told him about other places that souls may also choose as their spiritual training grounds. When souls choose earth, they know that they are facing certain hardships that they might not face elsewhere. Apparently, you have to be a hardy soul to survive here!

Past-Life Regressions

Trained hypnotherapists are able to regress (take backward in time) their clients in order to address personal issues and concerns. In the process of doing this, some hypnotherapists have discovered the past lives of their clients. One of them, psychiatrist Brian Weiss, MD, chronicled his experiences of discovering clients' past lives in his famous book *Many Lives, Many Masters.* He used hypnotherapy with many of his clients and one day stumbled upon a client's past life experiences by accident when, during a hypnosis session, the client began to recall and describe a past life.

Over time, the client recounted numerous previous lifetimes, and was able to identify people in her current life who had been with her in previous lives and in different roles. The client also began to share information that a "guide" wanted to tell the doctor. This guide told the client personal and extremely confidential information about Dr. Weiss' son who had died years earlier; she then shared that information with Dr. Weiss. Dr. Weiss says that there was no way this client could have known this specific information without having learned it directly from his deceased son.

It was that information, he says, that changed his beliefs about life after death. Knowing that his son's soul was still living on the other side was transformative for him, and it changed the trajectory of his life.

Following his experience with this client, Dr. Weiss began exploring past lives with several other clients. He wanted to share these experiences with his colleagues, but knew that if he did he would suffer ridicule and possibly even lose his license and his career. Ultimately he did take that risk, however, and has since become a best-selling author and public speaker. His work has helped countless people gain a deeper understanding of life and death, the immortal life of the soul, and the spiritual growth that occurs as a result of the sometimes difficult lessons we learn in this life.

Sometimes information from a person's past life helps to explain issues and symptoms that do not make sense in the context of their experiences or issues in this life. Think about your own life: if you were to list the issues with which you struggle, or the emotional or physical challenges that you face in your current life, you could probably trace them to experiences, illnesses, injuries, traumas, or some other aspect of your life. For example, if you struggle with depression, you might be able to recognize a family history of depression or bipolar disorder. If you have a bad back, you may know that it's from an old injury, arthritis, or poor posture. Or if you are afraid of dogs, perhaps you remember a frightening experience with them earlier in your life.

However, suppose you suffered from a terrible fear of choking, and you had no idea why. Could it be that in a past life, you were choked by someone or choked on something?

In his book *When the Impossible Happens,* psychiatrist Stanislav Grof shares stories of past-life interference in present-day life. Dr. Grof found that when clients were able to recall their past lives, they could pinpoint specific events that had "spilled over" into their present lives, causing their unexplained symptoms. This information enabled his clients to understand the symptoms, and ultimately for the symptoms to resolve on their own.

Leslie has struggled for years with a fear of fire. She has never had a bad experience with fire, but for as long as she remembers, she has feared it. She refused to even light a match until she was nineteen years old! Her fear had never made sense to her, and she wanted to know where it had originated. She hoped that this information could help her understand it and then let it go. She asked several people whose opinions she trusted and was given the names of reputable psychics who were in her general vicinity. Here's the story of what happened when she met with one of them:

> The psychic who met with Leslie told her that her fear had been caused by a terrible event in a past life. She said that Leslie's entire family had been killed in a house fire while she had been away, and that she had been understandably traumatized by it. She had felt enormous guilt for being gone when the fire occurred, believing that if she had been there, she could have saved her family. She felt responsible for their deaths, even though she could not have prevented the fire; it had been determined to be arson.
>
> Leslie's powerlessness to change what had happened led over time to her becoming first wary, then fearful, of fire in or near her home. She never lit candles or matches, did not allow smoking in her home, and did not store any sources of fuel in or near her home, for fear that they would ignite and cause a fire. In that prior life, she had not been able to shed her fear, and she had died still fearing fire and the loss that it could cause.
>
> The psychic explained that Leslie had brought her fear of fire into her current life, so that she could learn to face it and overcome it. This had been one of the tasks she had chosen to face in this life.
>
> Despite the skeptical voices within that told her psychics were full of nonsense, she felt deep down that the story was true. It resonated with something, some very faint memory or knowledge, inside her. And she felt immense relief. Her fear lessened substantially after this session with the psychic.
>
> But it did not go away completely, and she had to develop and utilize cognitive tools to remind herself that the dangers she perceived around fire in this life were actually remnants of a past

life—that if she used simple common sense and caution around fire now, she and her loved ones were not in danger.

Life Between Lives

Most spiritual teachers say that souls spend some time in between physical lives, during which they prepare for their next incarnation. It is a time of rest and renewal, reflection and decision. According to Michael Newton, PhD, whose books are based upon the reports of his clients during hypnotic spiritual regression, souls decide during this time what their purpose will be in the next life, and what lessons will be necessary in order to continue their spiritual growth.

Newton also says that souls rejoin their "soul groups," with whom they have been connected for many lifetimes. Members of the soul group, along with some advanced or wise elder souls, work with each soul to review its most recent lifetime, and to determine what spiritual lessons that soul wants or needs to learn in the next lifetime.

Most people "forget" their past lives and the lessons they have agreed to learn in their next life, so that when they enter the next life they will be able to fully experience the events that will teach those lessons. They are able to recall past life information under hypnosis because it bypasses the barriers of consciousness that keep them from remembering in their normal state of awareness.

Robert Schwartz, in his book *Your Soul's Plan: Discovering the Real Meaning of the Life You Planned Before You Were Born,* describes how souls decide to take on especially difficult or painful challenges in their lives and why they do so. He discusses challenges such as being born deaf or blind, having addictions, or being born gay or lesbian in a hostile community (regarding the latter, he suggests that souls decide on a lifetime of homosexuality because they want to strengthen their self-esteem by developing it from within, since it is not forthcoming from the outside in our society).

Lest it all sound heavy and serious, your life between lives is also a joyful time for rest, replenishing your energy, and reuniting with the beloved souls and spirit guides who have been connected with you throughout all your lifetimes. No doubt this is what some religious texts refer to as "heaven." For most souls, it feels like going home.

Michael Newton has trained people to do spiritual regression for others. His book *Life Between Lives* also offers thorough instructions for therapists who wish to do past-life regressions with their clients.

Toby Evans studied with Michael Newton and offers life-between-lives sessions and Akashic Record readings (you may recall that she was the healer involved in the Akashic Record reading in the previous chapter). She works from Sibley, Missouri, and both Cathy and Leslie have worked with her and recommend her to clients.

One of her clients, Jean Kilquist, wanted to share with us her life-between-lives regression story, and we are most grateful to her. This is again quite a lengthy story because of the amount of information that becomes available through a Life Between Lives (LBL) experience. Here is Jean's story:

> In 2010, I had an LBL hypnosis session with Toby Evans of *Sagebrush Exchange* (www.sagebrushexchange.com) in Sibley, Missouri. A few months before, I had read Michael Newton's book *Journey of Souls* and was enthralled by the thought that my life was one of many lifetimes my soul had lived over centuries. I went online to The Newton Institute website (www.newtoninstitue.org) and found Toby, the only Newton Institute-certified LBL practitioner in Missouri. Since I happened to already have a trip to her area planned, I emailed her on relatively short notice asking if she could do an LBL session with me, and she graciously agreed.
>
> At our session, I told Toby about my history, the important people in my life, and that my father had died a month before my tenth birthday. I was very close to him, and his death turned my world upside down. I felt I had to be strong, so I erected a sort of wall around me when my father died. I vowed that no one would ever know the vulnerability I felt inside my wall.
>
> Some years after I finished college, I became an over-the-road truck driver. There were almost no women driving solo at that time. As a college-educated female from upstate New York who

owned my own truck, I didn't fit into the culture, but I liked driving. After fourteen years on the road, I took an office job with the company. I have never married and have no children.

One night early in my driving career, I stopped at a NY Thruway Service Plaza known as Indian Castle. Two men came out to fuel my truck, one about thirty years older than I. I had an odd feeling that I was supposed to talk to someone there. When I visited the station three nights later, the older man came out again. That was when my life took a turn that changed everything for me.

The man's name was Harry, and he told me that he was the one I was supposed to talk to. Harry was Native American. He could *see* energy, and he said that when I had pulled in three nights before, he recognized my energy as identical to that of a girl he had been engaged to when he was a teenager. She had been murdered. He left his Cherokee community in Oklahoma after that, ending up in New York and pumping gas on the thruway. When I showed up, his entire world had been rocked.

Harry had studied to be a healer in his Native American community. Over the next two years, Harry mentored me in ways to use energy for health and protection. Then one day he told me I could not come to see him anymore. I took this as a rejection. What I didn't realize at the time was that Harry had taught me all he could, given me all the gifts he had to give, and he knew that it was time to turn me loose so I could move forward on my life's path.

During my LBL session, Toby hypnotized me and we worked backward through the years of my life, pausing at the day my father had died. I re-experienced that scene, as follows:

> *I am upstairs in my room, sitting on the floor. Toby asks me to describe my room, and suddenly I am more aware of the pattern on the linoleum than I had ever been while we lived there. My mother calls from downstairs, asking me to come down. There, I find my mother and two sisters (ages three and six) sitting on our couch. Our Lutheran minister, Pastor Gene, is on a chair facing them.*

I sit at one end of the couch, and Pastor Gene tells us our father has died.

My sisters are too young to understand at first what he's saying, but I get it right away. And, at that moment I know that life, as I have known and understood it, has changed forever.

My father was the parent I identified with, the one I knew loved me. I was not always so sure about my mother; she could be harsh with me. I decide, in a second, that I am never going to let anyone know this affects me in any way. I separate from the others and—in my mind—a huge steel door slams down, shutting my emotions off from the world. This is my secret.

While I was hypnotized, Toby facilitated a conversation between my adult self and the child I had been when my father died. I discovered that I had assumed the strong role and become the "man of the family" in his absence. Then my father tearfully entered the scene, explaining that he had not wanted to abandon me, and that his soul had been with me at several points in my life. His dying had been a part of both our spiritual paths.

I came to understand that his soul and mine were connected and that he would be sending me love from beyond—he wasn't really gone at all. I had been holding onto my father by always being strong, like a man is expected to be. I had cut off my innocence and vulnerability, and I needed to reclaim both if I wanted to live authentically.

From there, we went back to my most recent life, the one in which I was engaged to Harry, and was murdered:

I am barefoot, wearing a cotton skirt and blouse. My hair is dark, pulled back loosely at my neck, and hangs down between my shoulders. I am in a forest collecting plants, an assignment from my teacher. I am to find plants that will treat a certain malady. This is a test, and I feel confident that I know which plants are needed.

I take the plants back to my teacher and he is pleased. We're talking, and Harry comes in. He's a little older than I am. He and our teacher have sharp words. I think Harry wants to do something, and our teacher says, "No, you can't do that." I step back, away from the conflict. Harry thinks he has found a better way (he can be a little headstrong). Of course, from my teenaged perspective, and the fact that we are engaged, I think he is wonderful, intelligent, has good ideas, and is wicked handsome, but I also think he should do what our teacher says. Our teacher is an old shaman in a Cherokee community in northeast Oklahoma.

During my visit to this past lifetime, I was accompanied by a white light presence, a good energy that I recognized as familiar. I continued in that lifetime and witnessed my murder by a town drunkard. When he realized that he had killed me, he was horrified. I asked the white light presence, "Why did this happen? It is so sad for Harry and for the man who killed me." He answered that I had to leave so young in order to allow Harry to learn his life lessons. My being there would have kept him from doing so.

Toby was then able to call in Harry's spirit, who told me, "You know more than you think you do. It's in your right brain and you just need to open up to it."

We also called in my shaman teacher, whose heart had been broken when I was killed. He helped me to understand the brokenness of the man who killed me. I also felt the need to comfort my mother, who was very upset by my death. I wanted to ease her sorrow, so I whispered in her ear that everything would be okay. I was able to learn that her pain over my death became the greatest catalyst for her growth during that lifetime.

At that point, Toby took me to the "life between lives," the time between my former and my current lifetimes:

We pop through a ring of energy around the earth, and there are stars everywhere, and an energy pulling us. We reach the "arrival spot," and go through a brief "welcome home" ceremony with many others. Harry, the white light being, and I go to my soul group, which is along an energy "street." It's as if everybody who just came back is waving to one another, going back to their houses. It feels good to be here with all the energy, really nice. It's so nice to not be alone and not have to do it all myself. I haven't felt like this my whole life. I'm being greeted by a lot of smiles. "Hey. Where've you been? We've been waiting for you!" These people are happy to see me.

In my soul group, I see my mother, sisters, several friends, and my first boyfriend from 7th grade. Harry's soul vibrates at a higher level than everyone else, as does the white light being. Suddenly I am able to see who the white light energy is: it's the old shaman, my teacher from my past life! I ask him to guide me now to where I need to go next. I learn that he has been my teacher in many other lifetimes. He explains now that my purpose in this life is to become whole, to let in my vulnerability, to open my heart and accept myself. He and Harry suggest that I may even discover my soul mate (whom it turns out I was already acquainted with). The next several years of my life have the potential to be at the highest vibration of joy.

My LBL experience affirmed my life—the choices I had made, the path I had traveled. It confirmed for me the importance of my meeting Harry and my conscious decision to take him seriously. I saw that many small, seemingly insignificant things that I had done and experienced had actually contributed to the whole of my life's purpose. My years of trucking had enabled me to meet people who offered me words of wisdom, and some whose lives I enhanced as well.

With regard to my relationship with my father, I was gratified to know firsthand that he was not entirely gone, that I could connect with him when I wished, and that the possibility exists that I might encounter him in another incarnation at some future time. It was fulfilling to know how much he loved/loves me and how it hurt him to leave us as he did. Understanding that we had a soul contract helped me gain perspective about what happened. It didn't make it less painful, but at least easier to accept when I realized there was a higher purpose for everyone involved. I survived this loss, just as Harry and the old shaman survived losing me in my previous life.

With their help, I retrieved my lost inner child and that part of me that was sidelined in my previous life, bringing a younger perspective and joy into my current life. I am humbled that *two* advanced beings—Harry and the old shaman—both chose to incarnate with me and that they still interact with me regularly on other levels.

The LBL confirmed for me that I should follow my desire to become an energy healer in this life. I now do Reiki, Eden Energy Medicine, shamanic drumming, and Akashic Record readings. I still have my job in trucking, and I record a message every weekday morning that hundreds of drivers call in to listen to. I solve problems for them, and tell them to take care of each other and stay safe out there. I care about them, as I have lived on the road as they do. It's a small way of making their lives a little easier.

After-Death Communication

Sometimes souls on the other side contact people who are still living here on earth. Usually, they do this in order to help the person resolve a troubling issue or concern, or to reassure them in some way. Oftentimes the person's concern is around their relationship or experience with that soul when it was still incarnated on earth.

Such was the case with one of Cathy's clients, who had been struggling with the fact that her mother—who had died years earlier—had not protected her from the childhood abuse she suffered at the hands of her father. Cathy had been using Eye Movement Desensitization and Reprocessing (EMDR, a therapy tool we'll discuss in Chapter 13) with the client to help her process her memories and feelings about the abuse.

At the end of one particular session, Cathy was taking her client through a relaxation meditation in order to help her once again feel safe after remembering her trauma and feeling the emotions that went with it. As the client relaxed with her eyes closed, a look of shock and amazement crossed her face. Cathy noticed this, and watched as tears begin streaming down the client's face.

The client was silent for the remainder of the meditation. When it was over, she told Cathy that her mother had come to her during the meditation and apologized profusely for not having protected her from abuse. The mother had also shared how frightened she herself had been of her husband. This reconnection with her mother left the client with a profound sense of peace. She no longer felt upset with her mother; instead, she felt grateful to her mother for visiting her and helping her to heal.

In his work with military veterans, Dr. Alan Botkin used EMDR to help with war-related trauma. These clients often suffered from guilt and traumatic memories associated with having killed people during their tours of duty. Dr. Botkin was surprised when, during some of these sessions, his clients experienced spontaneous visits from the souls of people whom they had killed. According to the soldiers, the souls of the deceased came forward to let them know that they—those who had been killed—were okay, and that they forgave the soldiers for what had happened.

As you can imagine, these unexpected meetings were very healing for the veterans. Dr. Botkin has chronicled several of these encounters in his book, *Induced After-Death Communication*. Below, he shares the story of how he came to use this healing process with clients who were war veterans:

> I had been working as a psychologist on an inpatient Post Traumatic Stress Disorder unit at a VA hospital when Francine Shapiro published her first two articles on Eye Movement Desensitization and Reprocessing (EMDR). My colleagues and I were thrilled that we finally had a treatment that made a real difference. For the first time our combat veterans were able to

remember their traumatic events without having to relive them. Patients would routinely say things after a session like, "You know, Doc, this is the first time I feel like it's finally over."

Over the years I experimented with a number of variations of EMDR. While many of my ideas did not work, others seemed to make the process work even more efficiently. Therapy sessions routinely resulted in dramatic outcomes. It was a time of great optimism for me, my colleagues, and most importantly, for our patients.

When I began using one variation of EMDR that seemed very promising, something very strange began to happen. At first, I thought it was causing my patients to hallucinate, and I was appropriately concerned.

The first time this happened I was in a session with Sam, a Vietnam veteran. When in Vietnam, Sam developed a very close relationship with an orphaned ten-year-old Vietnamese girl named Le. Sam had plans to adopt Le and bring her back to the States with him. At the time Sam was not aware that the US government would not have allowed the adoption.

One day, however, orders came down that all of the orphaned children on the base camp were to be sent to a Catholic orphanage in a distant village. Sam and Le cried as he and the other soldiers were loading the children onto a flatbed truck. Sam promised Le that he would come and get her when he could.

Suddenly shots rang out and bullets were zipping over their heads. Sam and the other soldiers pulled the children off the truck and onto the ground as fast as they could. When the shooting stopped, and everything was safe again, they began putting the children back on the truck. They were nearly all on the truck when Sam noticed that he didn't see Le. He went around to the back of the truck and saw Le lying face down with a spot of blood on her back. He then turned her over and saw that a bullet that had entered her back had blown out her front torso. Le was dead.

In that moment Sam's life seemed to change forever. While in Vietnam he dealt with his profound sadness by covering it up with rage, and when he came home, he isolated himself in his basement and avoided contact with his own daughter, who triggered memories of Le's death.

After we processed his sadness with eye movements, and once he was experiencing a sense of relief, I gave him another set of eye movements. He closed his eyes, and I watched him as a broad smile came over his face. He silently sat with his eyes closed for a few minutes. When he opened his eyes he told me that Le had come to him as a grown woman in a beautiful white gown and with long black hair. She was surrounded by a beautiful white light.

She then privately said to Sam, "Thank you, Sam, for taking such good care of me back then." Sam then said to Le, "I love you, Le," and she responded by saying "I love you too, Sam." Le then reached out and gave Sam a hug. Sam said that he could actually feel her arms around him.

Sam was completely convinced that Le's spirit had just come to him, and he was joyous. I was concerned that his intense grief had compromised his psychological status. I was surprised to find out the next day that Sam was still in a great mood, and that there didn't seem to be any signs of psychological deterioration. In fact, after Sam went home on a weekend pass, he told us that he had made attempts to establish a relationship with his daughter. He said he was trying to "make up for lost time" with her.

I saw Sam over the next few weeks, and then over the next few months, when he would come back and visit the PTSD unit. The joy he felt in our session maintained. He said that every time he thinks of Le, he now has only "happy feelings."

After similar experiences happened with other patients, I went back to my notes to see if I had done anything different during the session. And, I saw it. After directly processing the sadness, and when patients were feeling relaxed and peaceful, an extra set of eye movements, without any suggestion, seemed to produce this very natural experience. I didn't know at the time that after-death communications, or ADCs, are not at all rare and occur spontaneously in at least 2 percent of the population.

Since then, I have further refined and developed a procedure that induces ADCs in a reliable fashion. I call it induced after-death communication, or IADC. Seventy-five percent of people who go through two sessions of IADC therapy experience a life-changing after-death communication. IADC has been growing rapidly over the years, and there are now IADC trained therapists in ten different countries. University research is also now underway in the United States. The Allan Botkin Institut, Deutschland opened in Saarbrucken, Germany a few years ago, and is devoted to IADC therapy, training, and research.

As a final note, it should be mentioned that I remain philosophically neutral regarding the issue of whether IADC experiences are spiritually authentic. As it turns out, it really doesn't matter what IADC therapists or patients believe, either before or after the experience. IADC works equally well with believers, agnostics, and atheists. The experience itself heals.

A Special Note Regarding Veterans

We want to add a special note here regarding soldiers and veterans, and the suffering that they so often endure as a result of their service. Soldiers are exposed to harsh conditions and life-threatening situations on a daily basis. The traumatic events that they experience and witness can create deep psychological and spiritual wounds. Many soldiers and veterans struggle with the belief that they should be strong enough to bear the pain of these wounds alone, and are reluctant to seek professional help.

As a result, the incidence of suicides among soldiers has risen sharply since 2005—according to Pentagon data, one soldier commits suicide every day. (Source: http://www. usatoday. com/news/military/story/2012-07-10/army-study-soldiers-suicides/56136192/1). It is vitally important that these men and women, who have sacrificed so much for their country, be gently guided to the help that they need and deserve. If you know a soldier or veteran who is struggling, suggest that they consider professional assistance.

The US Department of Veterans' Affairs employs therapists who specialize in helping soldiers and veterans with war-related trauma and other issues. EMDR may not be available at VA facilities, but many private practitioners do offer it. The EMDR Institute website (www.EMDR.com) can help you to find EMDR providers in your area. The Department of Veterans' Affairs can direct you to VA resources in your area; you can find information at http://www.mentalhealth.va.gov/ or call 877-WAR-VETS (927-8387). You can also contact mental health and psychological associations in your local area or state to find therapists who use EMDR and other trauma therapies.

The Bigger Picture

If you think about the kinds of issues you have faced during your lifetime, you know first-hand that earthly life can be difficult. Abuse, cruelty, greed, poverty, war, illness, loss, and other kinds of suffering cause us humans a lot of pain. If you consider that the hardships are a part of our spiritual advancement, that they teach valuable soul lessons, then the struggles can be seen from a different perspective. They become opportunities instead of unfair impositions of which we are helpless victims.

From our perspective as therapists (and having done a lot of healing on ourselves!), every traumatic event, every illness, and every troubling person who enters your life is there for your growth. Whether or not you chose it before you came into this lifetime, it is there for a reason, and you can learn from it. Finding the reason, making sense of the issues and the lessons that it brings, sets you free and helps you heal more quickly.

Sometimes a traumatic life event serves as a wake-up call that serves to bring you sharply into the present moment. You become more raw, more open, and your perspective shifts. It becomes crystal clear to you what is really important in life, and where you should put your energy. When this happens, you are suddenly more alive than ever before.

You may be wondering about life experiences such as abuse, murder, or other types of cruel behavior. Are the victims going through such trauma for their spiritual growth? We have struggled with that question as well. What we can tell you is that spiritual teachers, past-life regressionists, psychics, and astrologers say that yes, those experiences and other traumas are spiritual lessons.

Sometimes souls choose prior to a given lifetime to experience these things, despite the pain they will incur as a result. They do so in order to learn the spiritual lessons of those traumatic events, or to help another soul in their group or family to learn a spiritual lesson. The important thing to remember is that every spiritual lesson, even the extremely painful ones, is for the sole purpose of raising each soul's vibration in order to bring all souls closer to Divinity.

As our vibration increases and we advance to a higher energetic and spiritual level, our limited human ways of knowing and understanding are expanding as well. Gary Zukav sums it up nicely in *Soul to Soul:* "Humankind is now moving beyond the limitations of the five senses. It is becoming able to access data that the five senses cannot provide and to utilize that data consciously… Multisensory humans perceive physical circumstances, but they also see meaning in them that five-sensory humans do not" (p. 161).

13

When You Need Therapy

SOMETIMES, YOU JUST NEED a good therapist.*

The therapy relationship offers you the chance to feel heard, understood, and supported through whatever challenge you are facing. Sometimes that listening and understanding is healing in and of itself. There is evidence that a good therapeutic alliance can actually change and improve the structure of the brain. We still believe that, despite its limitations, therapy can be a useful and important component of healing.

There are some problems for which we believe that therapy is a must. You will find a list of these at the end of this chapter. We have also included a list of resources for immediate or crisis support. As a general rule, any issue that is long-lasting and/or that impacts your daily life is one for which you should consider seeking therapy. And if you are feeling like hurting yourself or someone else, you should seek help immediately.

But as we've discussed, traditional psychotherapy has its limitations. Issues that have an energetic or spiritual basis are sometimes not resolved sufficiently by simply talking through them. Likewise, our bodies store memory and trauma that may be experienced as physical pain, and they sometimes exhibit physical symptoms that are related to disruption in the flow of energy throughout the body. Past-life issues are sometimes

---

*Sign in at www.Spiritualprescriptions.com/bookbonus for a free report on how to find a therapist and how to avoid making the two biggest mistakes many people make when selecting a therapist.

involved in present-day problems, and unresolved issues with someone who has died may keep us stuck in emotional pain.

For these reasons, some innovative psychotherapy techniques have been developed in the past several years. Among them are Eye Movement Desensitization (EMDR), Thought Field Therapy (TFT), Psych-K (Psychological Kinesiology), and Sensorimotor Psychotherapy (SMP).

These treatments all focus on how memories are stored in the brain or in the body. Their common aim is to release trauma permanently by either moving it to a different area of the brain (EMDR), or by allowing it to move energetically through the body so that it resolves naturally. We will talk about each of these therapies in this chapter.

Eye Movement Desensitization and Reprocessing (EMDR)

Eye Movement Desensitization and Reprocessing (EMDR) works by moving traumatic or painful memory from the primitive part of the brain (at the back of the neck), to the frontal lobe (the forehead), so that it no longer holds its emotional power over us. When information is stuck in the primitive part of the brain, it is automatically triggered by any stimulation that remotely reminds it of the original trauma or painful situation. There is no thought or plan—it is just automatic.

This results in a "fight-or-flight-or-freeze" reaction, in which the person's adrenaline and cortisol start pumping through their body, their heart pounds, and their muscles tense in preparation to either freeze in place ("play dead"), physically defend themselves (fight), or run away (flee). Every nerve in their body goes on "high alert," and they startle at the slightest movement. This automatic fight-or-flight-or-freeze reaction is the mechanism behind the startle responses, flashbacks, nightmares, and chronic anxiety associated with post-traumatic stress disorder (PTSD).

Early humans needed this primitive mechanism in order to survive in the wilderness. They had to be keenly aware of their environment, for as much as they were predators, they were also prey to other animals. If a tiger suddenly leapt from its hiding place and prepared to attack, the human's brain had to leap as well—into immediate protective action. The primitive brain sent signals throughout the body so that all the mechanisms allowing fight, flight, or freeze responses would fire.

That primitive brain also needed to remember in vivid detail an image of that tiger: its appearance, smell, sounds, and a sense of its power to kill. The image needed to be linked with the immediate fight-or-flight-or-freeze response, whose emotional equivalent was fear. With the image and emotion freshly stored in the human's brain, any hint of the tiger's presence would trigger the memory and the fight-or-flight-or-freeze response.

As we have evolved as a species, our brains have retained this primitive alarm reaction to danger. The problem is that we rarely face tigers anymore. However, our brains are encoded with that response to any type of trauma or danger we encounter or perceive, so that all trauma memory is processed in this primitive part of the brain. There, the memory is flash-frozen, so to speak, so that it retains all of its emotional and physiological intensity, or "charge." This way, if we get even the slightest indication that the original trauma is going to be repeated, our fight-or-flight-or-freeze reaction is triggered.

Material that is stored in this part of the brain does not go through the normal memory processing channels in the brain. Instead, it stays there, ready to burst onto the scene at a moment's notice. This is why trauma memories seem so vivid, and why they have the emotional power to make us feel as though we are right back in the original traumatic situation. In order to move these memories through normal processing, we have to do something to get them moving.

EMDR accomplishes this using lateral eye movements to stimulate the material and move it from the brain stem to the frontal lobe. Once it is there, we are able to apply thought to it, to analyze the memory and come to the realization that the danger is not real in this moment. In other words, the process of moving memory to the frontal lobe strips it of its intensity, so that it can be recalled without the alarm reaction and emotional charge. The trauma happened long ago, is over with, and we survived it—otherwise we wouldn't be here remembering it.

Positive Emission Tomography (PET) scans of the brain before and after EMDR treatment indicate the change in activity in the brain from the brain stem to the frontal lobe.

EMDR can be very helpful in resolving symptoms of PTSD. It is also used to process unresolved grief, and has been successfully used to treat Obsessive-Compulsive Disorder (OCD).

Liz was a client of Cathy's who had experienced several traumatic events. She agreed to share this story of her work with Cathy using EMDR:

> Liz came to Cathy for outpatient therapy following one month in an inpatient treatment program. Cathy was the EMDR therapist on Liz's treatment team, which was additionally composed of a primary therapist, a psychiatrist, and a BodyTalk energy worker. Liz had been diagnosed with depression, an anxiety disorder, and alcohol dependence. In her case file were two full pages listing the numerous traumatic experiences that Liz had endured, starting at a very young age.
>
> Cathy initially worked on strengthening Liz's inner resources, those strengths and skills that she already possessed and that would support her through the painful feelings that might emerge during her EMDR treatment. She was understandably afraid of facing her traumas, and being assured of her internal and external sources of support helped to calm her fear.
>
> They began the EMDR treatment slowly, at a pace that was comfortable for Liz. Liz felt exhausted after her first session. After her second session, though, her distress level had dropped considerably. By the time of her third session, she was able to feel hopeful about her life—something she had not felt before that time.
>
> Over several weeks, Liz courageously faced the feelings she had locked away. She alternated between feeling rage toward her abusers and feeling positive about her life and her future. She started to notice that the anxiety that had been her constant companion was becoming less and less powerful. She felt sad when she recalled the lack of protection and support she had

received from her parents, but the sadness did not overwhelm her as it would have in the past. Liz grew increasingly aware of her own strength and resilience.

Liz was eager to know the context, or the bigger picture, in which her life had unfolded as it had. She had learned of a therapist in New Mexico, Shaina Noll, who offered comprehensive reports called Life Path Profiles. These reports explored a person's life from the perspectives of numerology, tarot, and astrology. Liz decided to order this report for herself. She brought it along to a session with Cathy, and read aloud the parts of it that felt particularly significant to her.

The section on Challenges stood out to Liz, and seemed to fit her life to a T. It described her life path, noting that she had "fears and undigested pain" associated with difficult experiences in the past, and said that people on this path were susceptible to falling into addictive and unhealthy patterns. It described such people as "late bloomers" in life, something that deeply resonated with Liz because she had often felt that she should have "had it together" much earlier in her life.

Liz's report also revealed that that very year was the one in which she "was expected to build her inner strength and bring forth new levels of courage, which would result in a new experience of enthusiasm and passion for the possibilities of life." This was an unexpected, positive affirmation for Liz. She was about to turn forty years old, and had been feeling like a failure. When she realized that she was right on time, that she was doing exactly what she should be doing, and that her years of empowerment were just ahead, she felt liberated and excited. Her Life Path Profile was such a gift to her!

Liz worked with Cathy for about one year, during which she processed trauma after trauma. With each piece of work, she felt herself grow lighter and more positive. Her anxiety dropped significantly. She demonstrated such courage and fortitude that Cathy felt honored to be able to watch as Liz stepped into her personal power.

Had Liz and Cathy merely talked through Liz's traumatic history, she likely could not have made such dramatic progress and would not have made it in such a short amount of time. *Traditional "talk" therapies do not address anything in the primitive part of the brain.* Talk therapy affects the frontal lobe, where normal memories are stored and the communication centers are. That part of the brain uses words and reason, neither of which is accessible to the primitive brain. But EMDR integrates this thinking part of the brain with the primitive brain, so that the person's healing is more complete.

It is important to note, though, that EMDR may not be suitable for everyone. People who struggle with Dissociative Identity Disorder (DID), in particular, are usually not good candidates for EMDR. Dissociative Identity Disorder most often develops over time, in situations where the trauma is ongoing rather than a single event. More trauma memories are created, and the intensity of so many memories emerging at once can be overwhelming for someone with this disorder.

All EMDR therapists should test you for dissociation prior to beginning an EMDR session. If you have a high level of dissociation (even if you don't have DID) and you do decide to try EMDR, it is imperative that you work with a therapist who is specifically trained to do EMDR with people who have DID.

Thought Field Therapy (TFT)

Thought Field Therapy (TFT) is a "tapping" technique that works by moving blocked energy through your body's energy meridians, or pathways, so that it can be released. This allows your body's energy to once again flow normally.

Think of it as similar to your digestive process: in order for food to be broken down and metabolized, it must be able to move smoothly through your digestive tract. If there is a blockage, the digestive process stops, food is not properly processed, and your whole system is disrupted. The solution is to remove the blockage so that everything can once again move smoothly.

Thought Field Therapy was developed by Roger Callahan, PhD (*Tapping the Healer Within).* It uses a prescribed series of taps on certain energy meridian "points" of the upper body and hands. Thought Field Therapy requires that you work with a trained therapist. It is an efficient system that effectively removes distressing or negative energy from your nervous system.

Psychologist Kathryn Ferner, PsyD (who offered an earlier story on the information given to her by a medium), uses TFT extensively in her practice, and provided us with this story:

> The woman was late for her appointment. It was her first, so I went outside to see if she was lost. Finding her, I brought her up to the office and asked her if she had had difficulty with the directions to the office.
>
> "Directions?" she asked. "I didn't have any directions." Shaking, she took her seat, handing me the required insurance form. I had sent her directions with the form, but didn't ask further.
>
> Short, light brown hair fell gently around a startled looking face. Quietly, I observed her as I took down some preliminary information and copied her insurance card. It was that "deer in the headlights" look that captured me—a trance-like quality to her movements and an empty gaze.
>
> I asked her why she had come. Her eyes immediately filled with tears as grief and fear overcame her. "I lost my third child," she said. "I was pregnant and there was a problem." Slowly, the story came out as she continued to shake. She did not seem to notice that she was crying. She had been six weeks pregnant when something went wrong. She was taken to the hospital for tests.
>
> Five and a half hours later, a medical team rushed in to inform her that immediate surgery was necessary. "There's internal bleeding" they told her. "We have to operate now. We don't know if you'll have a uterus when you wake up." There were other frightening things mentioned… She became further alarmed. She would lose the baby. Maybe there would not be a

chance of another. She had to understand this now before they put her under. She was shocked.

Six weeks later she was with me, recounting her story, the shock still apparent. She had been off work for the full six weeks, and it was becoming a problem at her workplace. Would she ever be able to work again? What would she do? What about another child? Barely spoken questions flitted around in her head like sparrows, never resting long enough to await an answer. Through it all, she shook.

Usually I wait for a new client to get used to me before I do any Complementary Medicine work. But she felt so desperate, so fragile, and was so in shock that I decided to test the waters. Slowly I introduced muscle testing, and asked at each step if we could proceed.

I explained PTSD and Thought Field Therapy and told her I thought it [TFT] would be helpful to her. She was ready to try anything. After she identified the trauma as a 10 on a scale of 0 to 10, with 10 being the highest, I asked her what the worst part of the whole thing was.

"I thought I was going to die!" she blurted. I asked her to focus on that thought. We did the TFT treatment, tapping in all the right places, until that trauma had been reduced to a rating of 0.

She was to return to her office for the first time the following Monday. After squeezing in a few extra minutes with her, I let her go with the request that she call me on Thursday if she was still feeling unable to go to her office. "This treatment should help, but I will work you in on Friday if you need it, and we'll decide then if you are ready to go back to work."

I checked messages on Thursday, but there was no call from her. I didn't hear from her for a while.

When she did make an appointment and I saw her for the first time since that memorable appointment, she came in with a smile and seated herself gracefully. I asked how she was, and she said she felt stressed.

"What's stressful now for you?" I was thinking of the trauma.

"Well, going back to work. There were a lot of changes and some people were in different positions and I had to get used to it."

"When did you go back?" I asked.

"Oh, well, you know, after I left here I felt so much better that I went and got my child from day care and took her to the office for my first time. I wanted to see people before I started back on Monday—thought it might ease the transition."

Stunned, I listened to her. I believed in the process and the work, and here was the evidence, yet again. Even though I had seen it before, each time took my breath away. There was no need to talk about the trauma for weeks or months. It was a single episode trauma, perfect for TFT, and her recovery was immediate. I felt so grateful for my training and the relief that TFT brings.

We turned our therapy focus to her current concerns—job stress. The PTSD was gone.

Psychological Kinesiology (Psych-K)

Psychological Kinesiology (PSYCH-K) is a therapeutic tool rather than an actual form of therapy. Only those professionally trained in its use can offer this technique, and it is sometimes used in the context of psychotherapy or counseling. We have included it in this chapter because it is effective and efficient.

PSYCH-K utilizes muscle testing to discover someone's "weak" and "strong" beliefs. It then helps to strengthen their positive beliefs. If you will remember, muscle testing involves placing gentle pressure on a person's outstretched arm. In this case, the tester asks yes-no questions (or makes true-false statements) while pushing down on the person's outstretched arm. If their arm falls to their side, it is considered a "weak" response and it indicates a "no" or "false" answer. If the arm remains outstretched to the side, it is a "strong" response and a "yes" or "true" answer.

For example, picture yourself standing with your arm held straight out to your side. You are facing another person, who says to you, "You believe that you are lovable." If your arm falls to your side when they lightly press on it, it means that you don't believe that you are lovable. If it remains steady, it means that you do believe it.

PSYCH-K is based on the idea that your beliefs establish the limits of what you can achieve. As Henry Ford once said, "If you believe you can or if you believe you can't, you're right!" The treatment is explained in the following summary, courtesy of the PSYCH-K website, at http://psych-k.com:

> Your life is a reflection of your beliefs. These beliefs—usually subconscious—are cumulative lifelong "programming." As a result of past negative programming, we sometimes think and behave in defeating ways. PSYCH-K provides a user-friendly way to rewrite the "software" of your mind and change beliefs that sabotage you, into beliefs that support you … quickly and easily … Using PSYCH-K techniques, "cross talk" between the two brain hemispheres is increased, achieving a more "whole-brain" balance, which is ideal for changing subconscious beliefs. In addition, when right and left hemispheres are in simultaneous communication, the qualities and characteristics of both hemispheres are available to maximize your full potential to life's challenges.

You will notice that with PSYCH-K, as with TFT, both sides of the brain are recruited in the process. This is important, really, for any form of treatment or therapy. Each side of the brain controls different functions and capacities, and when both sides "buy in" to the treatment, a more holistic healing can occur.

Our colleague Donna Montgomery, LISW, has used PSYCH-K to help several clients. One of her clients, Laura, felt extremely anxious about her upcoming wedding. Below, Donna shares the story of how PSYCH-K helped Laura to overcome her anxiety:

> Laura was a tall, model-thin brunette with jade green eyes, long dark lashes, full lips, and an easy smile. In other words, she was gorgeous! To look at her, one wouldn't suspect she was

consumed with anxiety, had low self-esteem, suffered from depression and felt she had to be perfect and to please everyone—except herself.

She and I had worked together for a year to help her heal from child abuse. Using standard psychotherapy, she had made good progress, her symptoms had subsided and she was nearing completion of her work.

During our time together she met a wonderful man, became engaged, and was soon to be married. As her wedding day drew near, many of her initial symptoms came bounding back.

She became quite anxious again, fretting over minor details, worried that the wedding wouldn't be perfect. Laura worried that she wouldn't be a beautiful bride. She couldn't stand that she would be the focus of attention. She was afraid she'd trip and fall going up the aisle, flub her vows, and bobble the dance with her new husband. She foresaw only disaster for the event she had long imagined would be the perfect wedding day.

As the wedding grew closer, she became tearful, couldn't sleep or eat, and worried continually. She felt desperate for something to help relieve her anxiety. I suggested PSYCH-K, and she agreed.

In only one session, we balanced for (strengthened positive beliefs for the client) the following:

- "I am a relaxed and peaceful bride."
- "I walk and dance with confidence and ease."
- "I relax and enjoy my wedding day."

Three weeks later, after the wedding and the honeymoon, Laura and I met again. She told me that the day of the wedding, she and her sister had been late getting home from having their hair and make-up done. The stylist had overdone her sister's make-up, and it had to be removed and reapplied. Her sister was very upset and almost in tears, knowing this would make them late for the photographer. Laura had calmed her sister and assured her that everything would be fine.

When they arrived at Laura's parents' home, the photographer had been quite upset about their tardiness. He was testy and insistent that they complete the photo shoot hastily, since they had scheduled a second session at a local park with the entire wedding party. Laura said that she had remained relaxed and calm through all of this, despite the photographer's tension.

After the first photo shoot, the photographer had been even more upset due to their running behind schedule. Laura was able to calmly talk with him and to assure him that it would all turn out fine. When they got to the park, the rest of the wedding party was noticeably anxious, wondering what had kept Laura, her sister and their parents from being on time. Once again, Laura said that she had felt relaxed and confident that everything would be fine. "Let's just begin taking the pictures," she said.

The photographer had just gotten the group posed when a bird flew over and unleashed his bowels on Laura's veil! While Laura's mother frantically tried to clean off the bird droppings, the photographer grew increasingly anxious and everyone in the wedding party was reduced to nervous laughter about the entire situation. Laura was able to truly appreciate the humor in the whole thing, and her laughter and relaxed demeanor kept the others in good humor.

Making it to the church with only minutes to spare before the start of the ceremony, Laura had felt calm and relaxed. She walked down the aisle with her father without a mishap. She said she knew all eyes were upon her, yet she felt beautiful, confident, and at peace. She said her vows without a mistake. The reception was perfect, from her first dance with her new husband through the rest of the evening. She greeted her guests in a relaxed and peaceful state and enjoyed her entire wedding day!

Laura did add that she wished she had done PSYCH-K for her honeymoon, as it would have helped to reduce her anxiety in response to missing their flight, lost luggage, less-than-desirable hotel accommodations, and a whopping sunburn to boot!

Trauma in the Body

Your physical body is intricately linked to your emotional health. There is no separation between the two, and disturbances in one cause disturbances in the other. For this reason, it is critical to consider your physical body in the process of any emotional healing. In terms of energy, the outer world is a reflection of the inner world. If you want to manifest abundance and well-being in your "outer" world, you must see to it that your physical body—the energy flow that governs all the systems therein—is in a state of health and vitality.

When working with clients who have been traumatized, as we did for years, we gained an appreciation for the idea "that the body never lies." It carries emotional pain and traumatic memories in its cells. We have witnessed clients, for example, whose physical bodies begin to show bruising, swelling, or other visible evidence of a traumatic event as it is being recalled in therapy. It is not uncommon for a handprint to emerge around the throat of someone who has been choked, or for a part of the body that was beaten to swell or redden as the client recounts the event.

This demonstrates just how closely aligned the body and the mind are, and it illustrates that the body remembers. Just as it is helpful to move memories from the brain stem to the frontal lobe, it is also important to allow painful memories to move through the physical body. Doing both allows memories to be resolved more completely than is possible with talk therapy alone. Trauma must be released from the body and the body brought into the present time.

As we explained with our discussion of EMDR, our primitive brain produces a fight-or-flight-or-freeze response in the face of perceived danger. For many years, this process was described only in terms of fight-or-flight; the freeze component is a recent addition. Freezing is akin to "playing dead," and this is a natural and automatic response when the threat appears impossible to escape or to resist by fighting.

You have likely seen this occur with animals—the "victim" or less powerful animal rolls over and becomes very still, sometimes actually feigning death. Animals do not want to eat "dead meat" that they did not kill. They know instinctively that doing so could be dangerous. So when prey are about to be attacked, they collapse and play dead in the hope that the attacking animal will walk away without killing and eating them. It is not a choice, but rather an instinctive response. Robert

C. Scaer outlines the evolution of our physiological response to fear and danger in his book *The Body Bears the Burden*.

We emphasize the automatic nature of the freeze response because so many survivors of trauma feel shame or self-loathing because they did not resist or fight the abuse in some fashion. They mistakenly believe that their instinctual survival response was a conscious and deliberate choice, or that they were simply too weak or lacked the courage to react otherwise. The truth is, the task of the victim of any trauma is to survive it. Period. And the primitive brain has built-in mechanisms to make that possible, one of which is to freeze or collapse. If you have experienced freezing or collapse in your life, it is imperative that you realize that *your body did not abandon you. It helped you to survive.*

From a physical perspective, humans get stuck in their trauma reactions when they don't get the chance to let their bodies do what they instinctively want to do in a dangerous situation. If an animal "freezes" to avoid attack, ideally the aggressor leaves the scene. And then what happens? The "victim" animal gets up and runs away as soon as it is safe to do so. It literally goes from its frozen physical position into an active series of physical movements that allow it to completely process the trauma. "Helpless and frozen" turns into "powerful and moving" when the animal flees the scene.

But this complete process does not usually happen with people. The trauma survivor often does not escape the attack. She may avoid being killed if she freezes or collapses, but she might still be assaulted. Thus, she does not get to complete the body's natural process of moving into action by fighting back or running away.

It is important to remember that not all trauma is a one-time event. Sometimes it occurs over a period of time, even over many years. It can consist of prolonged emotional abuse or neglect, as well as physical and sexual abuse that happened over months or years. Trauma may be hard to define or to pinpoint; you may not be able to point to specific events and say, "That was trauma." Instead, it may be a pattern of treatment, such as a parent consistently ignoring your emotional needs or telling you over and over that you are worthless. We use the term *trauma* to include both specific events and long-term patterns of behavior that have caused emotional wounds.

Helping the body to naturally complete the movements that were prevented at the time of the trauma can facilitate its letting go of the physical memory, which helps to heal the emotional wound as well. This is the focus of body-oriented therapies such as Sensorimotor Psychotherapy.

Sensorimotor Psychotherapy (SMP)

Sensorimotor Psychotherapy (SMP) considers the body to be central in the healing process. This therapy helps you to process trauma as it is stored in the body. You learn to be present in the moment, to observe and experience the physical sensations, patterns of movement, and "movement impulses" (the impulse to move in a certain way) that arise when you recall trauma. You are then encouraged to perform the natural movements that you were unable to complete at the time of the trauma, such as pushing the abuser away, physically protecting your body, or running away.

This process releases the physical energy that was trapped in your body at the time of the trauma, and this in turn creates a shift in your emotional reaction. The fear and helplessness of the past is resolved, and you feel empowered to develop new responses to the stressors that occur in your current life.

Ed Gutfreund, another of our colleagues, is a counselor, massage therapist, and Sensorimotor Psychotherapy practitioner. He agreed to share with us the following story of one of his clients:

> Stuart came to therapy because he was experiencing stress due to problems with his children. He had also lost both of his parents during the previous two years, and he was struggling with his grief. Shortly after we began therapy, though, he was surprised by the sudden memory of a sexual assault that he had experienced when he was young. This memory was very upsetting for him, and our therapy quickly changed focus to address this trauma memory.
>
> The first thing we did was to establish Stuart's resources—how had he successfully coped with stressful situations in the past? Who

in his present life was available to provide him with emotional support? We worked on helping him learn to "ground" himself by paying attention to his physical sensations; to literally feel his feet on the ground, to become aware of all that he was experiencing in the present moment. These were skills that would help him to feel safe and to soothe himself when he felt upset or afraid.

We used this present moment awareness to help him learn how his body reacted in the present to the sexual assault that had occurred in the past. What were his physical sensations? What happened with his muscles? What movements did he notice himself making? What movements did his body want to make?

Stuart noticed that when he recalled the sexual assault, he felt a sensation in his belly that he could not describe. He felt vulnerable. I asked what movements his body wanted to make, and he said that he wanted to curl up in a ball. I encouraged him to trust that impulse and to follow it. When he did so, I asked him what emotion came up. He said that he felt safer—protected. We noted that this could be a resource for him when he felt vulnerable.

When he came to his next session, Stuart no longer felt the impulse to curl up in a ball when he recalled the assault, but said that he felt hopeless and helpless when he thought of the assault. I asked him if he noticed any movement impulses, and he said that his hands wanted to curl into fists. I urged him to trust the impulse and to follow it, and he rolled his hands into tight fists. I asked him what movement impulse he felt next.

I have a big physioball in my office that clients use to help them express movements such as pushing and punching. It was right there in front of him, and I had told him beforehand that it was available if he wanted to use it. I asked him to follow the impulse to make the next move that his body wanted to make. He began to push it away from him at first, and as I encouraged him to perform the next movement and the next, he started to swing his fists at the ball and then to punch it vigorously.

I asked him what he noticed in his body as he punched, and he said that he could feel the strength in his muscles. When I asked what emotion he was feeling in that moment, he noticed

> that his helplessness and hopelessness had evolved into anger. He punched and punched until he no longer felt the urge, and afterward expressed great relief. By feeling his anger and allowing his body to release the energy of anger, he gained a new sense of his own power and strength.
>
> In subsequent sessions, Stuart was able to learn that his urge to push away what made him feel vulnerable was his body's way of setting boundaries. He discovered that while he could always protect himself by curling up in a ball—in essence, withdrawing—he could also begin to set boundaries and limits around himself. Doing so helped him to feel empowered and to assert himself, and this in turn allowed him to remain present and to interact with people instead of withdrawing to protect himself.
>
> And he had learned that if he ever needed to, he was capable of defending himself against danger. He recognized that he was an adult now, no longer the defenseless little boy he had been when he was assaulted. He felt grounded in his physical and emotional strength.

Stuart's experience with SMP demonstrates how body and mind are linked together with this treatment. As Stuart was able to integrate his body's natural sequences of movements, his emotions shifted and he was able to achieve new insights about self-protection, setting limits, and the strengths and tools he possessed as an adult.

SMP is also useful to help prepare you for future situations that are similar in some way to your original trauma. You can imagine some possible scenarios, then plan and rehearse with your therapist the actions, movements, and responses you would want to display in those cases. Planning and rehearsing like this allows you to "program" or encode the emotional and physical responses that would give you a sense of control and power in these situations. It also lets you practice feeling empowered, so your body and your mind become familiar with feeling and responding from your personal power.

We want to emphasize that none of this means that your reaction to the original trauma was wrong! Your only job in a traumatic situation is to survive, period, and whatever you did to survive was right and good.

SMP is simply a good way to help you become familiar with feeling positive and empowered.

A complete description of SMP is available in the book *Trauma and the Body*, by Pat Ogden, et al. By honoring the connection between mind, body, and emotions, SMP can help you achieve a deeper level of healing than talk therapy alone would provide.

There are many different theories and models of psychotherapy. Each one has its strengths and weaknesses. We recommend the models discussed in this chapter because they treat trauma and pain as it is stored in your body. This can lead to deeper healing than talk therapy alone is able to provide.

You Should Seek Therapy If . . .

These are situations for which you need—and deserve—extra support. You should seek therapy if:

- You feel like harming or killing yourself.
- You have tried to harm or kill yourself within the past year.
- You self-injure (cutting, burning, hitting yourself).
- You feel like harming or killing someone else.
- You are unable to function at work or at home.
- You are having frequent thoughts of dying.

Some situations are urgent, and require immediate action. If you are in immediate danger of harming yourself or someone else, please call 911 or go to the nearest hospital emergency room. In the United States, you can also call **1-800-273-TALK (8255)** for the National Suicide Prevention Lifeline, or **1-800-SUICIDE (784-2433)** for the National Hopeline Network. For help outside the United States, http://www.suicide.org offers crisis resources by country.

Please don't hesitate to get the support that you need. You are an integral part of this global transformation, and we want you with us for the journey!

14

We Are All One

SPIRITUAL HEALERS FROM MANY traditions recognize that we are in the midst of monumental, worldwide change. The process is intense, and everything is happening so fast that it can make your head spin! It can also feel scary at times.

Our planet is shifting and changing right along with us. Earthquakes, wildfires, tsunamis, global warming, severe drought, and epic floods are changing the surface of the earth every day. And by virtue of the fact that you are alive at this time, you are a part of it all. We urge you to trust that something wonderful is coming out of this metamorphosis. Your energy is being raised, along with all of humanity's energy, to a higher level of vibration.

Most of us fear change, and have no real concept of what it means to ascend to a higher level of vibration. Our human minds are limited, so we fear what we don't yet understand. Spiritual teacher and author Barbara Marx Hubbard likens us to caterpillars in the chrysalis, frightened that our lives are ending (*Humanity Ascending, Part 1: Our Story, 2008.* DVD). But we have nothing to fear. We will be creating together a new way of being, embracing our creative power and shedding the limited beliefs of our old, low level of vibration.

Our human minds have limited us and prevented us from seeing the Divinity in all of us. We have only recently begun to understand that we are creating our lives with our thoughts and emotions, and that we are all connected. It is our task now to embrace our creative power and to use it to create a world that is based on the principles of compassion, understanding, peace, and love.

How can we go about this task? We have to start by recognizing the old ideas that have influenced our thinking and our behavior—things like fear, power over others, competition and aggression, hate, intolerance, war, greed, the worship of material things, poverty, shame, and so on. All of these are toxic, low-vibration beliefs, attitudes, and actions, yet they have dominated our thinking for centuries. So how do we begin to change them? In these five easy steps:

> **Step 1**. The first real step is to recognize that all of these are our creations.
>
> **Step 2**. The second step is to realize that since they are our creations, we can stop creating them! Instead, we can start right now, in this minute, to create something new.
>
> **Step 3.** And in order for us to do that, we have to take the third step, which is to fully embrace our creative power and begin using it to create the world in which we want to live.
>
> **Step 4**. The fourth step is to remember our own Divinity. Our Divinity is God within us, and we must listen to that Divine voice in order to create our world. All the wisdom we need is right here, within all of us.
>
> **Step 5**. The fifth step is to come together to envision the world we want to create. Our combined, Divine wisdom has the power to manifest enough positive energy to fill the Universe! As we envision the new world order, so shall it be.

The Global Coherence Initiative

The Global Coherence Initiative (GCI) is an organization that was specifically designed to help us come together in the effort to create a positive new world. The people at the GCI describe their purpose in this way:

> This project has been initiated because millions of people sense that this is an extraordinary time; that we are at the crossroads of change and must move toward the healing of

> ourselves and our planet. Many people are feeling a strong desire to help change our present and future conditions and are looking for ways to use their heart, spirit-aligned wisdom and care to make a meaningful difference. The Global Coherence Initiative is a science-based, co-creative project to unite people in heart-focused care and intention, to facilitate the shift in global consciousness from instability and discord to balance, cooperation and enduring peace. (Used with permission from the Global Coherence Initiative).

GCI is an excellent resource and a way to bring together like-minded people from around the world who want to consciously create a better world. If you are one of these people—and the fact that you are reading this book suggests that you are—we encourage you to learn more about the GCI.

A New Paradigm

Our world has operated under the belief that the individual is more important than the group. From this paradigm have come aggression, greed, and the struggle for personal power. As the world experiences the turbulence of global transformation, we are being drawn into a new paradigm of concern for the total group, a need for cooperation, and an evolving belief that there is plenty for everyone.

We see the emergence of the new paradigm of cooperation in two recent examples. Both, ironically, involve competition, yet both display the energy of cooperation. In the first example, runner Oscar Pistorius was allowed to compete in the London Olympic Games alongside fully able-bodied runners, despite the fact that he wears prosthetic "blades" in place of legs. His request to do so was originally rejected by the Olympic committee because it had never been done before, and there was fear that his prosthesis might actually give him an unfair advantage over the other runners.

But someone finally agreed to investigate the situation, and it was scientifically proven that his artificial leg did not give him an advantage. In the place of rigid adherence to divisive rules, the spirit of cooperation emerged and enabled Oscar Pistorius to do what no handicapped person had done before him. He was warmly received by spectators and fellow athletes, who embraced and encouraged him.

The second example occurred in July 2012 at the Cincinnati World Choir Games. A choir composed of inmates from an Ohio prison asked to be able to compete in the Games. Because of their incarceration, they were not permitted to travel to the actual competition venue, and this could have excluded them from competing. However, the international panel of judges agreed to travel to the prison, a journey of almost 100 miles, to hear the choir and judge their performance on site. The choir was moved and so were the judges, and the choir's performance earned the gold medal for best male gospel choir. Cooperation and compassion moved hearts and changed minds.

In her book *The Secret History of Consciousness,* Meg Blackburn Losey shares her belief that "with our group consciousness focused on a joint goal, we can create a tidal wave of energies, all calling for the same outcome. And creation obliges" (p. 111). The stories of Oscar Pistorius at the Olympics and of the men's prison choir seed our imaginations with ideas of what is possible if we come together to co-create the new world.

With this in mind we want to share our last story with you. It is a true story, shared with us by transformational healer Lisa Michaels, whose program, Natural Rhythms (lisa-michaels. com), has been a life-changing resource for many people.

Lisa's story, from *Natural Rhythms: Connect the Creational Dance of Your Life to the Pulse of the Universe,* is a beautiful reminder that even when you are terrified, you can move into a state of all-consuming love. If each of us chooses to move into love over and over again as we walk through these turbulent times, the path into our new way of being will be much smoother.

> On a mid-summer day in 2002, while preparing for a talk on the elements, which I was giving the next day, I decided to go out in nature to go deeper into my own inner nature. I went to a beautiful mountain state park in Northern Georgia called

Raven Cliff. I stopped at the first campsite along the stream, which is just a short walk from the parking area. I spread out my blanket, made myself comfortable, then prepared to begin one of my favorite meditations.

First, I connected to Earth, my body, and the ability to bring things into structure and form in the physical me. Then, I connected to Water, the creek I was next to, my feelings, and the deep nourishment that comes from water. Next, I connected to Air and uplifted my thoughts and energy. I felt the sun on my face and connected to Fire and the life-force that flows through all things. I thanked Spirit for the opportunity to be there, and then I began my meditation.

The spot where I was sitting wasn't far off the path, and in the fifteen minutes I was sitting there ten to twelve people passed, talking loudly. I kept wondering if a quieter spot would have been a better choice, but I decided to stay where I was.

When I was complete, I walked to the water and stood facing downstream to ask Water to assist me in releasing old energy that needed to leave—especially old fears, feelings, and beliefs. Then I asked for something unusual. I asked Water to release me from anything that it felt needed to go that I hadn't considered. I then turned upstream to bring in the new and consciously opened myself to receive abundance, grace, and love.

As I was thinking about what else to open to, I looked across the stream and saw a black bear standing about eight to ten feet away on the shore ledge on the other side. A cub stood on the embankment behind her and a splash a little bit farther downstream drew my attention to a second cub in the water.

At once I moved into an altered state of awareness activated by a sudden adrenaline flood of fear rushing through my body. In the slow, dreamlike state of awareness in which I found myself, I believed the bear would just walk away on her side of the stream and all would be fine.

Instead, as I slowly began backing up, she started coming toward me. I called silently for protection and tried to remember what I'd heard about how to behave around bears. All I could remember was not to run. As she came across the stream, I noticed she actually had three good-sized cubs with her. I tried to stay calm and to slowly move out of her path, but she kept coming toward me.

Since I could think of nothing else to do, I decided to concentrate on opening my heart to send her love. I hid behind a tree, centered myself, and poured love not just to the bear and her cubs but into the whole area. She kept coming toward me, so I again backed up, while realizing there was no good way for me to maneuver out of the area without turning my back on the bears. I moved behind a larger tree and again poured love out of my heart toward her and the cubs, attempting to stay out of her line of sight.

At one point, I knew she was close to the tree and I wanted to know where she was, so I peered around the left side of the tree, only to find all three cubs were looking straight at me. I was entranced by how cute they were, but had to actively continue sending them love as I simultaneously experienced the most intense fear I had ever felt. I then internally said, "Spirit, the one thing I need this bear to do is to please leave the area." To my surprise, the bear then turned and walked off away from me, her cubs following behind her.

Next to witnessing my nephew's first breath and my sister's last breath, my encounter with the bear and her cubs afforded me the most amazing experience of the power of life and nature I have had to date. Looking that mama bear in the eye took me right to the fear of death. She could have decided I would make a good lunch, but fortunately she didn't. I am grateful that, in the time she was there, I was able to call on my ability to love—not just fear—and that she graced me so deeply with her presence.

Thanks to my work with the elements, I understood from Air how much my intention of "being protected" would assist me in the situation. I knew how much my vibration affects the world around me, and I realized that sending the bears the

> vibration of love was the only Power I possessed in that moment that could assist me.
>
> In addition, Water actively has taught me to choose love in the face of fear, and I was able to do just that during a time of enormous testing. Fire has been teaching me for years just how much personal power I have the ability to access. As four-legged animals that represent Earth, the bears gave me a direct experience of what happens to the world around me when I rise above my fear and walk in a space of love.
>
> Holding that much fear and that much love at the same time shifted something deep within me. I now truly know that each of us can choose to hold and send love in the face of fear. So many people think it is necessary to get rid of fear first before they can focus on love, but, in truth, you can feel the most fear you've ever felt and still choose to send love at the same time. (pp. 115-117)

In the wise words of meditation teacher Sharon Salzberg, " … a mind filled with fear can still be penetrated by the quality of lovingkindness. Moreover, a mind that is saturated by lovingkindness cannot be overcome by fear; even if fear should arise, it will not overpower such a mind." (*Lovingkindness,* p. 21).

There is no greater purpose in this life than to love. In *Your Soul's Plan*, author Robert Schwartz tells us that "Ultimately, the creation and expression of love in all forms is the very purpose of physical life" (p. 273). It is the theme of every report of a near-death experience, and it is the conclusion to which many people come as they draw nearer to death. Love is at the center of nearly every religious or spiritual tradition in the world. It is an emotion of the highest vibration.

You are a part of the cosmos, connected to everything and everyone in the Universe. At no moment and in no lifetime are you alone. And you have creative power to enable you to manifest a life—and a world—full of joy, abundance, and peace. But most of all, you are love, and you are loved.

It is our fervent prayer that people all over the world will use the ideas presented in this book to move beyond their emotional distress and to remember who they really are—Divine creators who courageously chose to be on this planet at this time.

We are the ones we have been waiting for, and together we can do this. It is no time to stay small or to play small. It is time to join together in our power and lift up the consciousness on earth for the benefit of all. We are grateful to all of you beyond words.

We are honored to be One with you.

Bibliography

Adyashanti. *True Meditation: Discover the Freedom of Pure Awareness.* Boulder, CO: Sounds True, Incorporated, 2006.

________. *Falling Into Grace: Insights on the End of Suffering.* Boulder, CO: Sounds True, 2011.

Amen, Daniel G., and Lisa C. Routh. *Healing Anxiety and Depression.* New York: Penguin Group, 2003.

Attwood, Janet Bray and Chris Attwood. *The Passion Test: The Effortless Path to Discovering Your Life Purpose.* New York: Penguin Group, 2008.

Botkin, Allan, R., Craig Hogan, and Raymond A. Moody. *Induced After-Death Communication: A New Therapy for Healing Grief and Trauma.* Newbury Port, MA: Hampton Roads Publishing, 2005.

Butterworth, Eric. *Discover the Power within You: A Guide to the Unexplored Depths Within.* New York: Harper One, 2008: xv, 66.

Callahan, Roger, and Richard Trubo. *Tapping the Healer Within: Using Thought-Field Therapy to Instantly Conquer Your Fears, Anxieties, and Emotional Distress.* New York: McGraw-Hill, 2002.

Carson, Richard David. *Taming Your Gremlin: A Surprisingly Simple Method for Getting Out of Your Own Way.* Rev. ed. North Yorkshire, UK: Quill, 2003.

Caudill, Maureen. *Suddenly Psychic: A Skeptic's Journey.* Charlottesville, VA: Hampton Roads Pub Co, 2006: 10.

Chodron, Pema. *Start Where You Are: A Guide to Compassionate Living.* Boston: Shambhala Publications, 1994.

Chopra, Deepak. *Life After Death: The Burden of Proof.* New York: Harmony, 2006: 267.

Cota-Robles, Patricia. *Who Am I and Why Am I Here.* Tucson, AZ: New Age Study of Humanity's Purpose, Inc., 2010.

________. *The Violet Flame: God's Gift to Humanity* (CD). Tucson, AZ: New Age Study of Humanity's Purpose, Inc., 2012.

Dooley, Mike. *Notes from the Universe: New Perspectives from an Old Friend.* New York: Atria Books/Beyond Words, 2007.

Dyer, Wayne. *Wishes Fulfilled: Mastering the Art of* Manifestion. Carlsbad, CA: Hay House, 2012.

Emoto, Masaru, and David A. Thayne, *The Hidden Messages in Water.* New York: Atria Books, 2005.

Frankl, Victor. *Man's Search for Meaning.* Boston: Beacon Press, 2006.

Friedlander, John, and Gloria Hemsher. *Psychic Psychology: Energy Skills for Life and Relationships.* Berkeley: North Atlantic Books, 2011: 69-74.

________. *Basic Psychic Development: A User's Guide to Auras, Chakras & Clairvoyance.* York Beach, ME: Red Wheel/Weiser, LLC, 1999.

Goldstein, Joseph, and Jack Kornfield. *Seeking the Heart of Wisdom: The Path of Insight Meditation.* Boston: Shambhala Publications, 2001.

Goodheart, George. *Applied Kinesiology.* 12th ed. Detroit: Privately Published, 1976.

Grof, Stanislov. *When the Impossible Happens: Adventures in Non-Ordinary Reality.* Louisville, CO: Sounds True, 2005.

Hanh, Thich Nhat. *Peace Is Every Step: The Path of Mindfulness in Everyday Life.* New York: Bantam, 1992.

________. *The Heart of the Buddha's Teachings: Transforming Suffering into Peace, Joy, and Liberation. New York: Broadway Books*, 1999.

Hay, Louise L. *You Can Heal Your Life.* Carlsbad, CA: Hay House, 1987.

Heriot, Drew, Sean Byrne, Darrian McLindon, and Marc Goldenfein (Directors), Rhonda Byrne, Bob Proctor, Rev. Michael Beckwith, Neale Donald Walsch, Jack Canfield (Actors). *The Secret*, [Motion Picture]. Luxembourg branch, TS Production, LLC, 2007.

Hewitt, William W. *Astrology for Beginners: An Easy Guide to Understanding and Interpreting your Chart.* Woodbury, MN: Llewellyn Publications, 1997: 16.

Hicks, Jerry and Esther. *Ask and It Is Given: Learning to Manifest Your Desires.* Carlsbad, CA: Hay House, 2005: 25, 47, 16, 114-115.

Hirsch, E.D., and Joseph F. Kett. *The New Dictionary of Cultural Literacy: What Every American Needs to Know.* New York: Houghton Mifflin Harcourt, 2002.

Humanity Ascending Series, Part 1: Our Story. DVD. Quantum Productions in Association with The Foundation For Conscious Evolution. Hubbard, Barbara M. (Featured Speaker). 2008.

Judith, Anodea. *Waking the Global Heart: Humanity's Rite of Passage from the Love of Power to the Power of Love.* Fulton CA: Elite Publishers, 2010.

Kabat-Zinn, Jon. *Mindfulness for Beginners.* Audio ed. Boulder, CO: Sounds True, 2006.

________. *Mindfulness for Beginners: Reclaiming the Present Moment—and Your Life*. Boulder, CO: Sounds True, 2012.

________. *Wherever You Go, There You Are: Mindfulness Meditation in Everyday Life*. New York: Hyperion Books, 1995.

________. *Full Catastrophe Living: Using the Wisdom of your Body and Mind to Face Stress, Pain and Illness*. New York: Bantam Dell, 1990.

Keyes, Ken. *The Hundreth Monkey*. Camarillo, CA: Devorss & Co, 1984.

Lipton, Bruce. *The Biology of Belief: Unleashing the Power of Consciousness, Matter, & Miracles.* Fulton, CA: Mountain of Love/Elite Books, 2005: 101, 84, 121.

Loyd, Alexander, and Ben Johnson. *The Healing Code: 6 Minutes to Heal the Source of Your Health, Success, or Relationship Issue*. New York: Grand Central Publishing, 2010: 220-224.

Losey, Meg Blackburn. *The Secret History of Consciousness: Ancient Keys to Our Future Survival.* San Francisco: Red Wheel/Weiser, LLC, 2010: 111.

Markova, Dawna. *No Enemies Within: A Creative Process for Discovering What's Right about What's Wrong.* Newbury Port, MA: Conari Press, 1994: 265-266.

McTaggart, Lynne. *Living The Field: Tapping into the Secret Force of the Universe.* Louisville, CO: Sounds True, Audio Learning Course, Six Discs, Unabridged ed., 2007.

________. *The Field: The Quest for the Secret Force of the Universe.* New York: Harper Collins Publishers, Inc., 2002: 115, 24, 26, 104.

Merton, Thomas, and Christine M. Bochen. *Thomas Merton: Essential Writings.* Maryknoll, NY: Orbis Books, 2000.

Mipham, Sakyong. *Turning the Mind Into an Ally.* New York: Riverhead Trade, 2003.

Michaels, Lisa Ann. *Natural Rhythms: Connect the Creational Dance of Your Life to the Pulse of the Universe.* Lilburn, GA: Institute of Conscious Expression Company, 2008: 24, 115-117.

Moorjani, Anita. *Dying To Be Me: My Journey from Cancer to Near Death to True Healing.* Carlsbad, CA: Hay House Inc., 2012.

Myss, Carolyn. *Why People Don't Heal and How They Can.* New York: Three Rivers Press, 1998.

Newton, Michael. *Life Between Lives: Hypnotherapy for Spiritual Regression.* Woodbury, MN: Llewellyn Publications, 2004.

________. *Destiny of Souls: New Case Studies of Life Between Lives.* 2nd ed. Woodbury, MN: Llewellyn Publications, 2000.

________. *Journey of Souls: Case Studies of Life Between Lives.* Woodbury, MN: Llewellyn Publications, 1994.

Noll, Shaina. *Songs for the Inner Child.* CD. Singing Heart Productions, 1992.

Ogden, Pat, Kekuni Minton, Clare Pain, Daniel J. Siegel, and Bessel van der Kolk. *Trauma and the Body: A Sensorimotor Approach to Psychotherapy.* New York: W.W. Norton & Company, 2006.

Remen, Rachel N. *Kitchen Table Wisdom: Stories that Heal.* New York: Riverhead Trade, 1997.

Roizen, Michael F., and Mehmet C. Oz. *You Staying Young: The Owner's Manual for Extending Your Warranty.* New York: Free Press, 2007: 187, 190.

Roman, Sanaya, and Duane Packer. *Opening to Channel: How to Connect with your Guide (Sanaya Roman).* Novato, CA: HJ Kramer, 1993.

Salzberg, Sharon. *Lovingkindness: the Revolutionary Art of Happiness.* Boston: Shambhala Publications, 2002: 17, 26, 20, 21.

Scaer, Robert C. *The Body Bears the Burden: Trauma, Dissociation, and Disease.* 2nd ed. Florence, KY: Routledge, 2007.

Schlitz, Marilyn M., Cassandra Vieten, and Tina Amorok. *Living Deeply: The Art & Science of Transformation in Everyday Life.* Oakland, CA: New Harbinger Publishing, Inc., 2007: 203.

Schwartz, Robert. *Your Soul's Plan: Discovering the Real Meaning of the Life You Planned Before You Were Born.* Berkeley, CA: Frog Books, 2009: 273.

Science of Mind Magazine. www.scienceofmind.com/faq.

Shapiro, Francine. *EMDR: The Breakthrough "Eye Movement" Therapy for Overcoming Anxiety, Stress and Trauma.* New York: Basic Books, 1998.

Sheldrake, Rupert. *Morphic Resonance: The Nature of Causative Formation.* South Paris, ME: Park Street Press, 2009.

Shinn, Florence S. *The Writings of Florence Scovel Shinn.* Camarillo CA: De Vorss, 1988: 8.

Siegel, Daniel J. *Mindsight: The New Science of Personal Transformation.* New York: Bantam Books, 2011.

________. *The Mindful Therapist: A Clinician's Guide to Mindsight and Neural Integration (Norton Series on Interpersonal Biology).* New York: W.W.Norton & Company, 2010.

Siegel, Ronald. *Mindfulness and Intimacy: Advanced Training in Relationship Building,* presented at the annual conference of the National Institute for the Clinical Application of Behavioral Medicine, 2010.

Suzuki, Shuntyu. *Zen Mind, Beginner's Mind: Informal Talks on Zen Meditation and Practice.* Boston, MA: Shambhala, 2011.

Talbot, Michael. *The Holographic Universe.* New York: HarperCollins Publishers, 1991.

Teilhard de Chardin, Pierre. *The Phenomenon of Man.* New York: Harper & Row, 1959: 32.

Todeschi, Kevin. *Edgar Cayce on the Akashic Records: The Book of Life.* Virginia Beach, VA: A.R.E. Press 1998: 2.

Tolle, Eckhart. *A New Earth: Awakening to your Life's Purpose.* New York: Dutton, 2005.

________. *The Power of Now: A Guide to Spiritual Enlightenment.* Novato, CA: New World Library, 2004.

Vitale, Joe, and Ihaleakala Hew Len. *Zero Limits: The Secret Hawaiian System for Wealth, Heath, Peace and More.* Hoboken, NJ: Wiley, 2008: 5, 41.

Weiss, Brian. *Many Lives, Many Masters: The True Story of a Prominent Psychiatrist, His Young Patient, and the Past-Life Therapy That Changed Both Their Lives.* New York: Touchstone, 1988.

Zukav, Gary. *Soul to Soul: Communications from the Heart.* New York: Free Press, 2007: 161.

Recommended Resources

Psychotherapists in Cincinnati/Northern Kentucky Area

Sue Telintelo, MSN, www.innerhealthcounseling.com, 513-793-4415
Donna Montgomery, LCSW, www.donnamontgomery.com, 859-292-8888
Kathryn Ferner, PsyD, 859-341-4480
Ed Gutfreund, LPCC, 513-319-4432

Psychics and Channelers/Intuitive Energy Readers

Julianna Kallas, www.juliannakallas.com, 978-468-1478
Karin Lubin, www.quantumleapcoaching.org

Astrologer

Pam Gallagher, www.midwestschoolofastrology.com, 513-984-2293

Psychic Healer

Gloria Hemsher, hemsherglo1@yahoo.com

Energy Healers in Cincinnati Area

Dave Dammert, Chiropractice Kinesiology, 513-791-3633
Melissa Hofmann, Cranial Sacral, Energy Therapies, 513-304-6176
Irena Miller, Reiki Master and SSR Energy, http://www.graceyogacenter.com

Massage Therapists in Cincinnati Area

Melissa Hofmann, 513-304-6176
Nita-Rose Augsbach, http://www.nitarosemassage.com/

Past Life Regression and Life Between Lives
Toby Evans, http://www.prairielabyrinth.com/

Natural Rhythms Trainings
Lisa Michaels, http://lisa-michaels.com/

Featured Websites

Cathy and Leslie's website, www.spiritualprescriptions.com

BodyTalk, http://www.bodytalksystem.com

Patricia Cota-Robles, www.eraofpeace.org

The Upledger Institute website (CranioSacral Therapy), http://www.Upledger.com

Panache Desai, http://www.panachedesai.com

Diamond Alignment, www.diamondalignment.com

EMDR Institute, Inc., www.EMDR.com

Jo Dunning, http://www.jodunning.com

Toby Evans (Life Between Lives and Akashic Record readings), www.sagebrushexchange.com

Happy Mother Coach, http://www.happymothercoach.com

Healing Touch, http://www.healingtouchinternational.org

The Healing Codes, http://thehealingcodes.com/

HeartMath, http://www.HeartMath.org

Jennifer McLean, http://www.healingwiththemasters.com

Mindfulness Based Stress Reduction, http://www.umassmed.edu

Michael Newton, www.newtoninstitue.org

PSYCH-K site, http://psych-k.com

The Pulse YouTube video, http://www.youtube.com/watch?v=E44bC8V3Ebo

Reflexology and massage therapy information, http://www.webmd.com/balance/massage-therapy-styles-and-health-benefits

Science of Mind, www.scienceof mind.com/

Soldier suicides story, http://www.usatoday.com/news/military/story/2012-07-10/army-study-soldiers-suicides/56136192/1

Suicide and crisis assistance outside the United States, http://www.suicide.org

Transcendental Meditation, http://www.tm.org

Veterans Mental Health, http://www.mentalhealth.va.gov

About the Authors

About Cathy Thomas

Cathy Thomas, LPCC, has a bachelor's degree in Honors Business and a master's degree in Educational Psychology from the University of Texas at Austin. She has over twenty-five years of experience in private practice as a psychotherapist specializing in post-traumatic stress disorder.

Cathy co-founded a holistic counseling center in Cincinnati, Ohio, where she employed many of the techniques and practices discussed in this book. She is currently retired and lives with her husband and two Australian Shepherds in Cincinnati.

About Leslie S. Evelo

Leslie S. Evelo, PhD, is a psychologist, Reiki Master, and founder of Online Therapeutic Consultation, LLC. She worked in private practice for twenty years, where she developed an interest in non-traditional and spiritual methods of healing.

Leslie currently works as a psychologist at the University of Cincinnati Student Health Services. She lives in Cincinnati with her life partner and her three dogs.

Permissions

We are very grateful to the many people who shared their very personal stories in this book. We also want to thank the people and organizations who have given us permission to reprint their material:

After-death communication story by Allan Botkin. Adapted with permission by Allan Botkin from his book *Induced After-Death Communication: A New Therapy for Healing Grief and Trauma*, Allan Botkin, R. Craig Hogan, and Raymond A. Moody, Hampton Roads Publishing, 2005.

Diamond Alignment biography and history. Used by permission of Jacqueline Joy and staff at www.diamondalignment.com.

Elements story by Lisa Michaels. Used by permission from Lisa Ann Michaels from *Natural Rhythms: Connect the Creational Dance of Your Life to the Pulse of the Universe*, Institute of Conscious Expression Company, April 2008.

Masaru Emoto photographs. Used by permission of the Office of Masaru Emoto, LLC.

Global Coherence Initiative section. Reprinted from www.heartmath.com and www.globalcoherence.org by permission of HeartMath.

God of the Heart Exercise. Adapted with permission by Gloria Hemsher from Chapter 4, *Basic Psychic Development: A User's Guide to Auras, Chakras & Clairvoyance*, John Friedlander and Gloria Hemsher, Weiser Books, 1999.

Grounding Exercise. Adapted with permission from Gloria Hemsher from Chapter 6 *Psychic Psychology: Energy Skills for Life and Relationships*, John Friedlander and Gloria Hemsher (www.psychicpsychology.org), North Atlantic Books, 2011.

The Healing Code by Alexander Loyd, PhD, ND with Ben Johnson, MD, DO, NMD. Foreword by Jordan Rubin, PhD, NMD. © 2011 by Alex Loyd. Used by permission of Grand Central Publishing. All rights reserved.

"You Can Relax Now" lyrics. Words and music by Susan McCullen. ©1986. Reprinted by permission of Heartland Publishing (BMI).